More praise for
Lady of the Northern Light

"Using fascinating rare lore from the north, this book unscrolls the inner meanings of the runes in a timely and provocative fashion. Whether used for divination or to better understand an earth-oriented culture, it offers a comprehensive new view of Scandinavian traditions."
—Patricia Monaghan, author of
The Book of Goddesses and Heroines
and *Seasons of the Witch*

"*Lady of the Northern Light* breaks new ground, showing the runes in their original aspects as symbols of the ancient Goddess of birth, death and rebirth. The author combines a deep sense of the sacred with an encyclopedic knowledge of folklore and myth."
—Miriam Robbins Dexter, Ph.D., author of
Whence the Goddess: A Source Book

LADY

of the

NORTHERN LIGHT

LADY

of the

NORTHERN LIGHT

A FEMINIST GUIDE TO
THE RUNES

Susan Gitlin-Emmer

The Crossing Press
Freedom, California 95019

Cover design by Sheryl Karas
Cover photograph courtesy of
The Central Board of National Antiquities
and the National Historical Museums of Sweden,
Antiquarian-Topographic Archives

Printed in the USA

Library of Congress Cataloging-in-Publication data

Gitlin-Emmer, Susan
    Lady of the northern light: a feminist guide to the runes/Susan
Gitlin-Emmer
        p.   cm.
    Includes bibliographical references.
    ISBN 0-89594-630-0.   —ISBN 0-89594-629-7 (pbk.)
    1.Runes — Miscellanea. 2. Goddesses — Scandinavia — History.
3. Goddess religion.   I Title.
BF1779.R86G57   1993
133.3'3—dc20

                                  93-5281
                                  CIP

Acknowledgments

I offer gratitude and appreciation to a great many people both for their friendship and their support during the course of writing this book. Among them, Pat Monaghan, for sharing my passion for a Goddess who was the sun, and for endless letters, phone calls and visits devoted to discussing Her, as well as the pleasure of doing workshops together; to Miriam Dexter, for long lunches, answering my questions about etymology (any mistakes are my own), and reading the first version of the book; to Geraldine Hanon, for introducing me to the Macintosh!!!, for having been through the process of writing a book and convincing me whenever necessary that I really could do it too, as well as for astrological advice; to Sandra Golvin, for thinking of the title, for years of being a terrific "art buddy," for phone conversations that both fed me and kept me grounded, and for loving encouragement and advice; to Starr Goode, for endless phone calls, referrals, insight and understanding.

A big thank you and warm hug to Maureen Murdock and Diana Rico for the benefit of their experience and advice as writers. Thanks to Anne Gauldin for long talks and the view from Machu Picchu, and to Judy Stock for clarity of mind and our weekly writing sessions. I extend my gratitude to The Crossing Press and my publishers, John and Elaine Goldman Gill, for their belief in my work. Thank you also to Barbara Beattie for her expert proofing of the manuscript.

The practice of Witchcraft is central to my life and my work. To the women with whom I share both: my coven sisters in *Nemesis* (Ruth Ann Anderson, Anne Gauldin, Cheri Gaulke, Starr Goode, Kathleen Forrest, Sue Maberry, Christine Papalexis) and *The Angel Girls* (Sandra, Geraldine, Miriam) for family, rituals, inspiration and magic, a heartfelt thank you and my love. Two women from my very first circle also deserve special thanks: Alberta Maschal, with whom I first found the Craft and thus began this journey, and Donna Goldstein, who did the beautiful drawings that are part of this book. I owe special thanks as well to all my students in Feminist Wicca who helped to convince me of the need for a feminist view of the runes and encouraged me to write it.

No book about the Goddess could be written without acknowledging the debt we all owe to Marija Gimbutas for restoring to us so much of our past. For both her work and her friendship, I offer my thanks and my love.

Special thanks go to Fred Emmer, who has always believed both in me and the work, and who provided unfailing love and support. A big hug for my son Josh, who helped me remember to return to the present when I got too deeply immersed. To our two cats; Lessa, for patiently keeping me company no matter where or when I decided to write, and Kimi, for reminding me to eat by finding me and demanding to be fed.

Susan Gitlin-Emmer
Autumn Equinox, 1992
Reseda, California

*To the Great Goddess
in all Her manifestations.*

*May we feel in our bones
the touch of Her magic.*

Table of Contents

Guide to Finding the Runes

Guide to Finding the Runes

Preface

My first encounter with the runes was accidental. While doing some research on ancient Sun Goddesses, I was reading the material available from Scandinavia, with its traditional belief in a female sun. Looking through some material on the runic alphabet, more or less in passing, I discovered that the sixteenth rune, Sowilo, stood for the Sun Goddess Herself. I was hooked. Everything I had ever read about the runes spoke of them as a late Indo-European development and tied them to the God Odin. What was the Sun Goddess doing in the middle of an alphabet supposedly sacred to a warrior people worshipping a sky god? Whether She was from some other source, or a vestigial remains of the Proto Indo-European Sun Goddess, how had She come to remain a part of the sacred alphabet? Her presence demanded a closer look. As I studied the accepted meanings for other letters of the Elder Futhark, the oldest form of the runes, I felt a kind of vertigo. Here were all the same symbols I had learned to associate with the Goddess and Her diverse aspects and Epiphanies.

The Meldorf brooch, found on the west coast of Jutland and dated from approximately 50 CE, represents the oldest object discovered with runic writing in the Elder Futhark. Prior to around 200 CE, there is evidence of use of the Elder Futhark in the area that is present day Denmark, southern Sweden and southeastern Norway. The alphabet in its entirety appears only on a standing stone found in Kylver, Sweden, and dated at the fifth century CE. As a tradition, runic writing lasted until around 1000 CE, but the Elder Futhark faded out about 800 CE.[1] There does not seem to be general agreement among scholars as to its origins, but the most widely accepted theory is that it developed from a northern Italian (Etruscan) alphabet. Mythologically, we are told that Odin received the runes by hanging upside-down on the tree of life for nine nights.

All sources seem to agree that the primary function of the runes was magical and religious. There is a strong similarity between certain runes and Bronze Age (1600–450 BCE) ideographic rock carvings found throughout Scandinavia. Is it possible that the mysteries of the Great Goddess, originally transmitted in rock carvings and oral tradition, had led to the development of a "Goddess language" that had simply become associated at a much later date with the new runic alphabet? The familiarity of its symbols may have been responsible for the runes' widespread acceptance in Scandinavia. By re-examining the runic alphabet, could we then recover an ancient Scandinavian view of the Goddess and Her world?

This is what I have set out to do. Some of the runes were immediately accessible as representations of the Goddess with which I was familiar from other parts of the world. This familiarity, after all, was what had first attracted me. Others were buried under a vast overlay of Indo-European mythology and Christianity. Among the literary sources available is a collection of poems written by different poets at different times known as the Elder Edda (or Poetic Edda). The usual date attributed to the majority of the works is the tenth century CE. A second source is the Prose Edda, written by an Icelander, Snorri Sturluson, and dated at approximately 1220 CE. Sturluson's work retells many myths and refers to still others that are lost to us. Sturluson himself was a Christian. The third source is from approximately the same time and consists of a many-volumed work in Latin by the Dane, Saxo Grammaticus. He gives us Danish versions of the myths, exploits of heroes and religious practices.

Taken together, these sources constitute most of the written material available to us about pre-Christian Scandinavia. Yet they are only a source of late Indo-Europeanized beliefs at a time when Scandinavia was primarily Christian. Other sources of information include the work of early historians, such as the Roman accounts by Tacitus. While Scandinavia remained Pagan until around the tenth century CE, the vast trade routes and numerous invasions meant that a great many peoples had contributed bits and pieces that influenced the few written sources of mythology we have available to us.

Still, certain themes began to grow clearer. Each rune represented a cluster of related ideas, together weaving a picture I could begin to identify. I came to this work both as an artist and a modern priestess of the Goddess. As an artist, I was able to work intuitively with the symbols that appeared at first most obscure, and to trust my instincts that certain concepts were related to ones I was familiar with in other regions, which in turn often led to new areas of research. As a priestess, the Goddess cycle of life/death/rebirth, embodied in the changing cycles of nature, is one with which I am intimately familiar. Even across such a vast stretch of time and generations, and complicated by the rich diversity of traditions, Her footsteps were familiar ones.

Introduction

The oldest form of the runes, called the Elder Futhark, contains twenty-four letters. While those letters each had a phonetic value, their primary use and meaning were always magical. How can we come to know the magical meanings and uses of the runes today?

There is no ancient text in existence to give us those meanings. What we do have are several old rune poems—Icelandic, Norwegian and Anglo-Saxon—that have verses for each of the runes then being used. None of these poems used all the letters of the Elder Futhark except the Anglo-Saxon Rune Poem, which had four additional letters. Most rune interpretations have depended heavily on this poem. The Anglo-Saxon Rune Poem reminds one of Robert Graves' work in *The White Goddess* with "The Song of Amergin," so much lies in the reconstruction and interpretation.

No matter what sources we turn to for inspiration and understanding, the end result is colored by what we expect to find. The basic, often unstated assumptions of a researcher about the subject being researched influence how that research is interpreted. All of our interpretations of the runes up until now have been dependent on the idea that the runes were a product of the time period during which the inscriptions appeared. Thus, the runes have been understood as a phenomenon best viewed in the light of Viking culture. Given that basic assumption, they must be seen as patriarchal. We, as a far distant but also patriarchal culture, have not questioned this greatly. Yet, suppose that they are older. Not the runes themselves, but the concepts behind them. Suppose that the very reason the runes caught on in Scandinavia was that the concepts connected to them could be related to already accepted ideas, those of a Bronze Age Goddess and Her world and symbols. Thus, in much the same way that Mary was accepted because She was seen simply as a new name for existing local Goddesses in many parts of the world, the runes were not regarded as an entirely foreign belief system as they traveled north from Italy. This is clearly a different assumption than we have made about them in the past, and it opens up new possibilities.

What if we add one more thing to our working assumptions— that is, that the meanings associated with the runes changed over time. There can be little doubt that by the time Scandinavia had finally embraced Christianity, the myths and symbols of an older time had been affected. Let's look at the stories of the Eddas themselves. They tell us that with the coming of the Aesir, the shape of the previous pantheon of Scandinavian Goddesses and gods was altered. What if we attempt to go back farther, to a time before either of those pantheons? Most scholars agree that at one time the Goddess Nerthus was of far more importance than Her consort. Many also feel that Her "daughter" Freya was once of far more importance than Frey. Certainly there was a time in the Bronze Age (which like everything else came late to Scandinavia) when there was a Goddess who was the most important deity. All the literature leaves to us is hints. What is left are Goddesses of different names and specialized domains that even traditional scholars often feel may have once been aspects of a more powerful Goddess—as Horn, Mardoll, Gollveig are all aspects of Freya. If we begin our journey with the assumption that such a Goddess existed, then we can examine what survived of Her into historical times with a different perspective.

If we take this as our starting point as we look at the runes, what do we have to go on? First, of course, there are the rune names themselves. Each rune has come to have a traditional meaning attached to it. Often that meaning is open to more than one possible interpretation. The same is true of traditional source material such as the Eddas; much of what we find depends on our initial assumptions. Then we can look at similar symbols or ideas as they survive in folk customs and fairy tales, always remembering that these, too, change over time. We can even look at similar concepts in other parts of the world for hints, as long as we remember how vastly different meanings can be in different places. Scandinavia was part of a vast network of trade routes from early in her history. Ideas came with that trade and left with it as well.

The runes did not exist in a vacuum. While each rune had a separate meaning and use, they were all part of an attempt to magically describe not only the Goddess, but the underlying world view held by the culture in which She was celebrated. Each rune is discrete, but only to a point. What did this culture look like? What can we discover about the Goddess the runes reveal?

While we may never know either Her original name or origins, it is clear that both Nerthus and the later Goddesses of the Eddas are Her descendants. She was a deity of the full circle of life/death/rebirth. In all probability, as Nerthus, She was a Triple Goddess and Her other aspects might have been Ingun and Skadi.

She was the All Giver. Her spirit dwelled in mountains, stones, wells and streams, caves and sacred groves. We see Her in the runes as the needle ash and the birch tree, but other trees were sacred to Her as well, among them the yew, elm and elder. She was the cycle of the seasons in turn. She brought the buds to the trees in spring and was the source of all wealth, fertility and abundance. Daffodils rose up where Her feet passed, and She left Her footprints on the rocks as She danced the circle of life. The growth of crops and their harvest were Her gifts. Fire was sacred to Her and Her people used it to call on Her to bless their crops and help them in times of need. She was the sun in the sky and Her radiance brought renewal. Gold and amber were Her tears and blessings. She was the Mistress of storms, and the blanket of snow and ice that came to the land each winter. She was the great weaver on whose celestial spindle the world turned, and She brought to humankind the gifts of flax and weaving. She was the Death Goddess whose balance was necessary for the survival of life. She rode on the back of the wolf with a bridle of poisonous snakes. She was Queen of the Dead, and She led the Wild Hunt. Hers was the womb, cave, cauldron of rebirth. She was related to the most ancient Bird Goddess and at some point was owl, raven, swan and goose. Her Epiphanies included the cow, the snake, the reindeer, the sow, the mare and the fish. Horned animals, such as bulls, boars and goats, were sacred to Her. She was the source of inspiration and the foundation of all wisdom. She was the mother of gods and of humanity. She was the source of all magic and prophecy, of songs, words and history. Her sexuality was a source of pleasure and mystery, sacred and awesome in its power.

This is a Goddess akin to the Old European Great Goddess, if not Her reflection. Her presence in the runes argues that She held sway in Scandinavia for a very long time, even after Her name had been forgotten and Her powers fractured and dispersed among Her many daughters and the patriarchal gods that claimed Her place. Through the runes we can once again see Her revealed in all Her majesty and vision.

Accessing Your Own Wisdom

In Western culture, logical thinking is valued far above intuitive thought. This societal preference for left brain over right brain thinking means that many of us have only limited access to the creative potential inherent in right brain spatial, intuitive perception. In addition, we sometimes disregard the messages we do receive from this part of ourselves. This is the part of our mind that is most aware of connection and relationship, of our interwoven pattern in the fabric of the universe. The runes can be used as a tool to deepen our awareness. As we use this side of ourselves more fully, we can begin to integrate both kinds of perception, both ways of knowing. This is the key to accessing our own deep wisdom.

The runes are a tool for self-knowledge. They help us to see how we make choices and changes in our lives, to explore our strengths and our weaknesses, to open to our own creative potential. In the world of the Goddess all things are interrelated. The runes help us to gain the perspective necessary to see our place in that vast web. They can also help us to see how the choices we make affect both ourselves and the web. The runes bring no answers from an outside authority. Instead, they help us to consult the deep wisdom we all possess. The Goddess is immanent in each of us. We each choose how we will manifest Her wisdom.

The Rune Journal

One of the best tools for working with the runes is a journal. If you already keep a journal, you may wish to add the impressions gained from working with the runes to your daily entries. How does the rune you have drawn relate to the rest of your entry? If you aren't a journal keeper, you may still find a rune journal useful.

Begin by recording the date, the issue (if specific) and the rune(s) you have drawn. Briefly record your impression about each rune and any insight you have as to how it relates to your daily life. You may want to record your impressions visually. Over time you will develop a set of associations that help you recognize how the energy of the runes interacts in your life. This will be your best guide to interpreting the runes' purpose in any given situation.

As you work with each rune, work first with the feelings and sensations it calls up for you. Record these impressions as fully as possible—even if they don't appear to make logical sense! Record any images that come to mind in as much detail as you can, using all your senses. Then look at the section on the rune or runes you have drawn. Ask yourself how the situation, questions, feelings, that it brings up are operating in your life. Again, record your impressions.

You can gain still more from your readings by reviewing your journal entries. Go back over your journal once a week. Do comments that didn't quite make sense fall into place? Can you see new meanings as your perspective changes? Date your weekly review and try writing it in a different color pen. At the end of the month, go over your weekly reviews, just as you had your previous entries. Do you see a pattern? Has a particular rune or several runes come up repeatedly? Again, date your monthly review and use a different color with which to write. At the end of the year (or in between if you feel the need), you can review the monthly

10

summaries. You don't have to work by the calendar. I find it easier and more meaningful to review the entries in my rune journal at each full moon, and review my full moon entries at Samhain.

There have been times in my life, such as while working on this book, when I used the runes daily. Then there were times when I used them only when I felt the need. When you first begin to work with the runes, frequency of use will help to turn them into a tool you can rely on when you need them.

Working with the Runes

To begin you will need a set of runes. A wide variety of possibilities exists. You might begin with a store bought set, or you might make your own. In either case, keep in mind that there were many different runic alphabets. Even within an alphabet, there were often variations in some symbols. To use this book effectively, you will need a set of runes marked with the Elder Futhark, the runic alphabet that I discuss.

The right set of runes is the set that you feel is right for you, the one to which you are most drawn. You may even find that you want to have more than one set, using them for different things. Runes are available in a growing variety of forms. The tactile quality of the set you choose is important as well as the visual qualities. Remember that in using the runes you will be holding and handling them a lot. Pick a set that feels good to touch and is easy to hold. Keep in mind that you will be working with twenty-four runes, so avoid runes that are too large to handle comfortably. I find that a set that I can fit into one hand is the easiest to use.

Wood, stone and clay are the most common materials used. If you are buying or making a set from wood, there are a few things to consider. Some traditions say that runes should be made from a branch of a fruit-bearing tree. Two other woods associated with divination are the elder and the rowan. Runestaves were also made of yew. Before you decide on a particular type of wood, you might want to read about it. Look up the lore connected with it. What parts of the world is it found in? What are its magical significances, if any? But ultimately, trust the associations and feelings you hold for a particular wood and let them determine your choice.

You can find rune sets available marked on all types of stones—everything from polished or tumbled beach stones to sets of semi-precious stones such as rose quartz or amethyst. You might enjoy learning some of the history and mythology connected with the kind of stone you are considering. Rose quartz, for example, is used to amplify one's capacity for self-love and acceptance. It would be particularly appropriate if your primary purpose in using the runes was self-knowledge. You can mark your own runes on stones using a diamond point stylus (such as those used for etching). Another possibility is to look for stones, perhaps along the ocean or at places that are special to you, whose markings resemble a particular rune. This process could take a long time, but the set it yielded would be unique.

One of the easiest ways to make a set of runes is from fired clay or from one of the many forms of modeling clay available, that can be finished without a kiln. These can be painted or stained, or the clay itself can be given color by adding things to it. One of my favorite sets of runes is made from modeling clay to which I added earth from sacred places and rituals.

As you work with the runes over time, you will develop your own rituals. Remember, rituals speak directly to younger self. They are a way of telling yourself what it is you are about to do and what you expect of it. They create a sense of expectation that helps to reinforce the work you will do with the runes. There are no "correct" rituals. What works is what is right for you. You will need somewhere to keep your runes, first a bag or box to hold them and then a place to keep it. When I am working with my runes regularly, I keep them on my altar.

The easiest way to purify your runes is with incense. Move the incense over the runes in what the Native Americans call *smudging*. Use an incense appropriate to your purpose, such as lemon, cedar or sage. But runes can also be purified by simply shuffling them. Keep your intention firmly in mind and visualize them being cleared as you shuffle.

A good way to begin working with the runes is to set aside fifteen or twenty minutes at the same time each day. Try to make the place where you will work conducive to the kind of work you are about to do. You might begin by lighting a candle on your altar and end by drawing or recording your insights. The runes can be used as part of a daily meditation, or to create affirmations for yourself. Use whatever methods you normally do, to ground and center yourself. Let go of any tension or worry. You may wish to cast a circle before you begin. Be sure you feel safe and protected. In this way you will be free to open yourself most fully to the reading you are about to do. If you decide to draw a rune at a time when you are unable to do any preparation, it can still be effective. The most important thing you bring to your work with the runes is intention. Ritual is an aid to moving that intention from intellectual purpose to a deeper level.

Before you draw a rune, clarify the issue you want to work with. Are there several choices involved? What is it that you would like more information about? The clearer you can be about the issue, the clearer your answers will seem. If you are deeply concerned with one issue, you may find that the runes you draw relate to that issue, no matter what question you ask. Be clear about your intention; it is that which will guide your choice of runes.

The easiest way to work with the runes is to have a bag large enough to hold your runes with enough room to reach in and draw one out. Shake the bag to shuffle the runes. Consider carefully what issue you want to consult your deepest self about, and hold that intention in your mind. Reach into the bag and draw a rune. For a daily reading, your question might be: What do I need to be most aware of? or What should I remember to bear in mind as I move through the day? Relating to the issues in your life through the use of the runes helps to put them in a wider perspective. Through the runes you can become clearer about the choices you make and the way in which you live on the planet.

Rune Layouts

The simplest layout, and the one I use most often, is the three-rune spread. Although it is a simple layout, it allows for a great deal of variety and can be adapted to most situations. You will probably want to experiment with it a bit to find how it works best for you. You are going to be using three runes. You can draw them from the bag one at a time or spread the runes out face down and draw three. The order in which you lay out the runes is up to you. Some people work in a line, moving from left to right, some from right to left. I usually arrange them in a triangle. But no matter how you decide to place them, you will have three positions. *Before* you start, decide how you will place them and in what order. Does the first rune you draw go at the top of the triangle or the right side? Whatever you decide—stick to it! The three-rune spread has its parallel in the Tarot. If you are used to working with the Tarot, the same designations you use for a three-card spread will work equally well for the runes.

There is a wide variety of things that a three-rune spread can represent. For a daily journal spread, the runes might be: the challenge the day will present, the mode of action to deal with it, the lesson to be learned. Here again, the important thing is to be very clear about what each position means *before* you begin, and then to stick to it.

Some variations I have found useful include:

past → present → future

issue → right action → outcome

situation → obstacle → pathway

child self → logical self → inner wisdom

Another simple layout is based on the Celtic Cross. The rune in the center indicates the issue or situation with which you are dealing. You may draw a rune for this position or pick one you feel describes it best. Or you may find you want to do both. In that case, the rune you select represents your conscious view of the issue and the one you draw is an aspect you aren't taking into account. Then, beginning to the right of center and moving clockwise, draw a rune for each of the Quarters: East, South, West and North.

The rune in the position of the East represents the beginnings of a project, idea, relationship or that which forms the heart of it. It is also your mental attitude toward the issue, the perspective from which you view it, the place where clarity is most needed. The South represents the fire that fuels the issue, your desire and will at play in the situation, and sometimes the obstacles that will have to be overcome. The West represents your feelings and emotions with regard to the issue, connections to the past, old issues that are related, your hopes and your dreams in the situation. The North is whatever the issue is grounded in, the root of a situation, the mystery that it evokes, the wisdom to be learned from it.

Even if you are unsure about the way to interpret a particular rune, continue to work your way through the reading.

If any of the runes that you draw present you with obstacles or predicaments, you can shuffle or mix the remaining runes again and draw another rune for that direction. Ask for clarity, wisdom or whatever additional help that direction has to offer. Generally, one additional rune is all you will find useful.

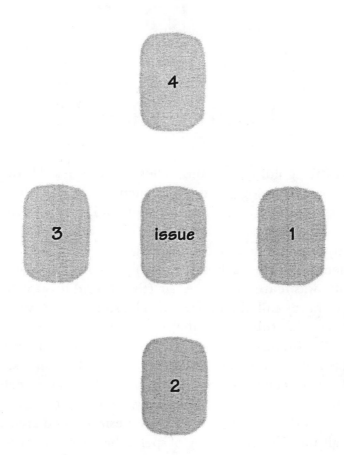

When you begin to work with the runes, you embark on a journey to your inner self. Trust both yourself and the process and you will be changed by it. The runes are a tool that connect us not only to ourselves but to a Goddess oriented world and culture similar in many ways to the Pagan world today. As such, for many of us, they are a particularly appropriate tool for self-exploration.

1. Fehu: Riches

Fehu is cattle, gold, wealth, the riches of the runes. Throughout Scandinavian mythology, gold is associated with the Goddess. Freya cries tears of gold. Sif has hair made of gold. The phrase "Goddess of gold" is a metaphor for women. One of the first Goddesses of consequence in the Eddas is Gollveig or "gold might." Gollveig was a member of the earliest group of gods and Goddesses, the Vanir. She was feared by the Aesir (the second group) for Her magic, and they called Her a witch. The story of Her visit to the Aesir tells us that three times they tried to burn Her in the fire in Odin's hall.[1] But this was one witch whose magic was too strong for them. Each time She emerged from the fire whole and shining. From this She received a new name, Heid, the bright or shining one.[2] The Eddas tell us that eventually, after a battle that sprang from the Aesir's treatment of Her, the Aesir learned Her magic. This magic included the casting of spells, the use of trance and the use of wooden wands in divination—the reading of the runes.[3] Thus, truly the riches of the runes belong to Fehu and the Goddess. Most scholars consider Gollveig to be an aspect of the Goddess Freya. Both Freya and Her sister Goddess Frigg were considered seers. Their ability to prophesy is part of Fehu's wealth.

Gollveig was tested in the heat of the fire and, like gold itself, came from it purified and shining. The fire was Her element. This fire is related to the luck bestowed by the rune Fehu and the Goddess in Her aspect of good fortune, the smiling side of the Goddess of Fate. Fire is often associated with luck; because of this association, it is important that the fires of the Goddess not go out, lest Her luck go as well. There were perpetual fires in temples throughout Scandinavia.[4] We know that the fires in the temples of both the Irish Bridget and Roman Vesta were carefully guarded and considered to represent the luck of the community. In Ireland, to give away fire for any reason on Beltaine is still considered giving away your luck for the year.[5] In *The Golden Bough,* Frazer tells us that deities associated with perpetual fires are often seen as the source of sunshine.[6]

Gold and fire are also associated with three other Goddesses and heroines of the Eddas. They are described with *kennings* (metaphors) of light and gold, and each one is found in a place surrounded with a circle of light and fire. (Svipdagsmal surrounds the hall where Mengold is secured; Skirnnismdal surrounds the abode of Gerd; and Signdrifumal surrounds the mound where Brynhild is held in magic sleep.) Such rings of fire are associated with fairy hills and with tomb mounds, both of which are gateways to the underworld. Like Gollveig rising from the fire of Odin's hall, the force implied here is the power of regeneration or rebirth.

One of Freya's primary symbols is the famous necklace, *Brisingamen*. The word comes from the Old Norse *brisingr,* "fire" and *men,* "necklace" or "girdle," thus also a ring of fire.[7] The myth in which Freya acquires the necklace by first spending one night with each of four dwarfs, whose names are the four directions, is seen by some as a metaphor for the traveling of the sun through the solstices and equinoxes. The necklace is created in the fire of the dwarfs' forge. Many examples exist of Scandinavian Bronze Age Goddesses. They are usually portrayed naked except for a small band or girdle, arm bands and a necklace.

Wealth in an agricultural society often meant cattle. Marija Gimbutas tells us that the descendants of the ancient Snake Goddess who represented "fertility, abundance and well being" were often cow-faced like Hera or Hathor, or associated with cows like the Celtic Verbeia or Bridget. She also tells us that one of the most persistent symbols of the Snake Goddess was a crown, that symbolized wisdom, often accompanied by vegetation.[8] We can see the persistence of such beliefs in Scandinavian folk customs. In Germany, some time in September, the cattle are returned from their mountain pastures by the girls who herd them. They deck the cows with flowers and adorn them with two-tiered wooden crowns.[9] In Norway, on Mikkelnesse (September 29), herd girls also drive the cattle and goats home from the mountain farms decked with flowers and with much rejoicing. The summer camps are operated by women, usually the eldest daughters.[10] Julaften (Winter Solstice) decorations in Norway include crowns plaited in straw.

There is a Norwegian folk tale of a girl who forgot to feed a cow over the Winter Solstice. The cow wished her blind and she was.[11] Blindness is a curse also inflicted on mortals by fairies seen dancing in their fairy rings. Similarly, mortals who saw the Goddess Nerthus in Her bath were drowned. Nerthus is one of the oldest Scandinavian Goddesses that we know by name, dating from the Bronze Age. She was invoked by farmers to bring gifts of cattle in the spring. In some parts of Scandinavia, She was also called Huldra. In this form, Her maidens were "wood nymphs." They looked like women dressed in long white robes, but could be recognized by their cows' tails hanging below the hems. Huldra and Her maidens protected the cattle while in their mountain pastures and sang magic songs, sometimes heard by wandering mortals.[12]

By whatever name we know Her, this is a powerful aspect of the Goddess. She enters your life bearing riches. Fehu may manifest as physical wealth—gold, cattle; or as luck in whatever you are bringing into being. The face of Fate that the Goddess shows in Fehu is shining. But Her riches may take other forms as well. She knows what is to come. Her gift is also that of divination, the touch of prophecy. This is the rune of psychic gifts and knowledge. Hers is the power to pass through the fire purified and strong, rich in experience. Honor and petition Her with fire and shining things. Burn candles to Her on your altar. Call on Her when you would read the runes. To call on Her is strong magic. Remember to honor and thank Her for the blessings She sends your way.

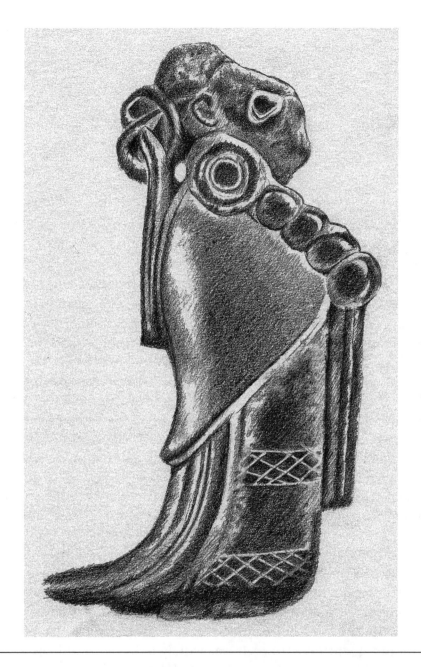

A sixth century CE silver-gilt pendant from Uppland, Sweden, shows Freya, with her hair in a stylized knot, wearing Brisingamen.

2. Uruz: Aurochs

Uruz is the energy of the new form manifesting, the energy of the Goddess that gives shape to the universe. The ability to manifest energy as form is the essence of magic. It is represented by the horns of the aurochs, a large wild ox, once found across most of Europe. The shape of the rune suggests these long, curved horns.

In Old Norse, the rune took on a new name and meaning: Ur or drizzling rain.[1] One can see the suggestion of rain in the shape of the rune as well. The association between the ox and the rains that bring seasonal rebirth to plant life is an old one. It is as old as the Paleolithic when we find the aurochs painted on cave walls, along with abundant plant life. The walls of seventh millennium Catal Huyuk were also painted with aurochs. Below the shrine floor, aurochs skulls were found as burial goods, accompanied by eggs, grain and figurines of boars.[2] The use of the ox or bull as a sacrificial animal was widespread. The Eddas tell us of the sacrificing of oxen to Freya, and of spreading their blood on the stones of Her altar.[3] In this instance the energy of the ox was used to stimulate the Goddess' own energy to bring forth. It was thought that the blood of a bull would bring new life to the earth as late as the nineteenth century.[4] It was widely believed that bees were formed in the body of a sacrificed bull by spontaneous regeneration. The birth of new life came from the body of the sacrificed bull, or by extension, from its blood, and like the drizzle, the soft spring rains, brought about the cyclical greening of the earth. Both the aurochs and the drizzle were seen as symbols of Her transformative energy. It is for this reason that the name of the rune could change without significant change in meaning.

The aurochs was one of Her sacred animals because it represented the strength of Her life-forming energy. Other horned animals also represented this energy of formation. Their horns, or tusks, particularly curved ones, were energy symbols. Thus boars, deer, rams and goats were also sacred to Her. The shape of their horns was seen as relating to the waxing and waning of the moon, and the spiral journey of the sun—the patterns of creation. Uruz does not dictate the form new life will take; rather, it makes it possible for this new form to manifest. It is the tendency of all life to follow the pattern of the diacosmos.

Aurochs were also part of the animal processions that appeared on cave walls from the Upper Paleolithic and represented life forming and transforming in cyclical time.[5] The most familiar of such processions is the zodiac. They appear, as well, in procession on pottery from many countries. In Malta, they form a particularly beautiful frieze on the stone of the temple of Tarxien. As later myths reveal to us, here is the Lady of the Animals in a series of seasonal transformations. She is the hunter and the hunted, the fish and the net, the source of life and of death. Her story reappears in many parts of the world with interesting variations. At first all the transformations are Hers as She moves through the year. Then She chases a vegetation god around the year, catching and devouring him.[6] According to Tacitus, the earliest Scandinavian god is Tvisto, an earth or vegetation god. Male energy was primarily associated with the rise and fall of seasonal vegetation in Scandinavia. Each successive god till Odin, including Frey and Thor, was a year god of vegetation. In Sweden, at May Eve, there was a ritual enactment of a play called *Bukkerwise*, where a goat (sacred to Thor as the boar was to Frey) was mated to the Goddess, sacrificed and reborn.[7] Finally, as the Indo-European gods dominated, She is chased around the seasons by a god who attempts to catch and rape or marry Her, until She escapes by a final change of form.[8] (See Othala.)

A well known example of this type of tale is "The Romance of Taliesin," where Gwion is eaten by the Goddess as the Hag Cerridwen, and reborn from Her cauldron as Taliesin. She pursues him as they both change shape in a seasonal round: dog after hare, otter after fish, falcon after dove, and finally hen after the corn.[9] The seasonal procession of animals represents the solar year and the journey through it. There are several notable variations of this kind of transformation cycle that survive in Scandinavia.

One version of this mythological chase is from a twelfth century tale in Saxo Grammaticus' *History of Denmark*. Aslog, daughter of Brynhild, lived on a farm in Norway. She was disguised as a kitchen maid with Her face covered with soot or ashes (part black and part white), named *Krake* or Raven.[10] Odin's raven must have originally belonged to Freya, even as Apollo's sacred bird, the crow, belonged first to Athena.[11] Despite Her disguise, the hero was taken with Her and set Her a test to determine if She was worthy of his love.[12] She must come to him "neither on foot nor riding, neither dressed nor naked, neither fasting nor feasting, neither attended nor alone." She arrived riding on the back of a goat, one foot trailing, wearing Her hair and a fishnet, an onion to Her lips, a hound at Her side.[13] She is the Maid who is also the Hag, neither one thing nor the other, the energy of life that transcends form. Holda was said to appear on May Eve riding a goat accompanied by twenty-four hounds. She was often shown as piebald— part black, part white—as was Hel, for they were "twins," or the same Goddess in Her aspects of Hag and Maid[14] (black raven and white swan). This was sometimes simplified as Love (sexuality) and Death: the odd combination of traits that remains to Goddesses like Freya. Freya, to whom oxen are sacrificed, who rides a boar or in a carriage drawn by two cats, rules the Valkyries with their raven form and has a falcon cloak that allows Her to fly, is obviously a part of this tradition. Were Freya's ravens the same black birds as those in the hymn to the Goddess Hel that became a nursery rhyme?

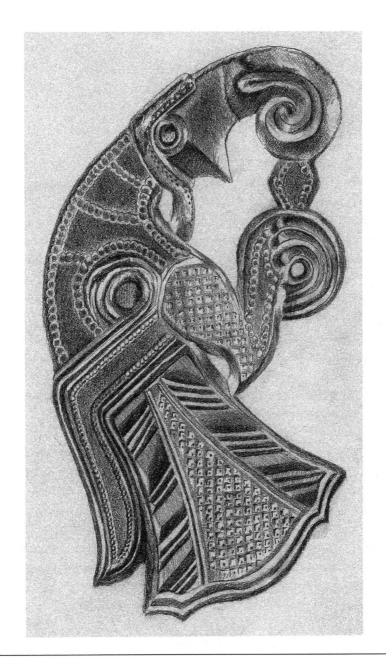

A stylized bronze raven, with spiral claws and beak from Gotland, Sweden.

Four and twenty blackbirds,
baked into a pie.
When the pie was opened,
the birds began to sing.
Wasn't that a dainty dish,
to set before a king?

They were birds of prophecy. They sang of the king's impending death (or of the death of the goat that would be sacrificed in his stead) and rebirth, as all vegetation gods were reborn in spring, when the Goddess emerged from the hill or sun maze of winter. But they were also the sacred alphabet of the Goddess that held Her mystery. At one time (before that mystery was rearranged to fit the letters of the runes that would both hide and preserve it), it may have represented a sacred seasonal calendar as well.

As we turn the wheel of the seasons, each form must give way: flower becomes fruit becomes seed. The corn must be cut to provide the harvest and next year's crop. Even the sun in its triumph at the Summer Solstice must give way to the growing dark. She is the energy behind form, constantly changing but never lost. We, as all Her children, are one with the endless procession of all life.

The aurochs and other horned animals represent Her energy. It is a source you can draw on to create change, to work magic. But it must be directed with clear purpose and intent to be effective. Uruz is a rune of transformation and it can manifest in many ways. To change shape, you must become one with the form you would take on. When you draw Uruz, you are in touch with the common threads that weave together all life. Honor the energy of the Goddess in whatever life form you find it. Know that each form has its place in the diacosmos and something it can teach us.

3. Thurisaz: Giant

The giant one. The good one. The giants predated the gods of
the Eddas. They were thought of as the first life to come from the
cold of the far north. As the enemies of the Eddic gods, they were
also seen as ugly and evil.[1] Likewise, by the time of the Anglo-
Saxon rune poem this rune became known as *thorn*, an evil thing.
But the Gothic word for this rune was *thiuth*, the good one. The
Old Norse name *Thurs* meant giant.[2] The giants of the Eddas had,
as a group, a variety of names. The name *Thurses* may have meant
thirst (as in the thirsty ones) or it may have come from *turseis*,
meaning high towers.[3] If so, what were these towers, and why were
they related to the giants? There is very little Scandinavian material left to tell us, but there are interesting hints from neighbor-
ing parts of the world.

One of the late associations with this rune was with the hammer of Thor, an Eddic god and particular enemy of the giants. The
hammer later became associated with this rune,[4] but in fact it was
probably the freeing of the sun from the bonds of winter that was
the older association. There is a Lithuanian tale about the worship of a huge iron hammer. The hammer was said to be important
because once the sun had disappeared for several months, locked
in a tower by a king. The sun was freed by the signs of the zodiac
with a huge hammer.[5] This is a tale with obvious northern origins, where indeed the sun does not appear in the sky for over a
month in the dark of winter. The hammer could have been a con-

stellation that rose at about the time the sun would reappear. It is interesting to note that the constellation we know as Orion was once called Thor.

In the Midsummer festivals and processions of France, Belgium and England through the last century, very tall structures made of osiers or wicker work and called giants, were moved through the streets. Sometimes they were burned in the bonfires. Sometimes the structures were not giants, but towers. They were filled with animals (serpents, cats, foxes) or decorated with flowers. Frazer sees these towers or giants as representatives of the corn or tree spirit, and their burning as a form of sympathetic magic to bring sunlight and fertility to the crops.[6] Once again these towers or giants associated with them were linked to the need to increase the powers of the sun.

As the good one, Thurs brought about this renewal. The sun began to regain its strength at the Winter Solstice. The celebration of Yule was sacred to Freya, who returned from the south riding the boar Ottar (sunshine) and brought with Her the time of spring. Thurisaz is also seen as the power of regeneration and fertility.[7] On Scandinavian Bronze Age rock art, sows and boars also appear, along with spindles, distaffs and sun symbols. Pat Monaghan considers one carving at Ostergotland to be that of a distaff spinning a sow.[8]

The pig or sow was one of the oldest forms of the Goddess. Pigs were sacred in Crete.[9] Suckling pigs were offered to Demeter and other grain or bread-giving deities at harvest time. The pigs were thrown into a pit or cleft or sacred cave, representing Her own womb and the underworld into which She descended as Persephone. There the carcasses were left to rot, accompanied by bread and pine boughs. Serpents dwelling in the caves ate some of the offering. Later they were placed on the altar and included in the spring sowing to increase the fertility of the seed and crops. In Her sow form She was invoked as protection for the crops from such things as foul weather. Ritual eating of the pig was a part of Her worship. In eating the pig, Her worshipers partook of its vitality, and sacramentally ate of Her flesh.[10] The Swedish custom of "dipping" is still practiced on Christmas Eve. Fat from the Yule pig is rendered and the vitality of the pig is believed to flee into the fat. It is then poured into a pot, and bread is dipped into it with all partaking.[11]

In Norway, pigs are slaughtered in November and made into sausages to be served at Christmas. When sliced, the sausages reveal patterns of stars or spirals.[12] In Sweden, the bones of a pig must not be split or gnawed until just before New Year. Then they are saved until the spring sowing and scattered in the fields.[13] Likewise, at the feast of Yule, the main dish that graces the table is a roast pig with the apple of rebirth in its mouth. This is accompanied by breads baked in the shape of sunwheels and deer, and by cheeses carved in the same images.[14] There is a custom common to both Sweden and Denmark of baking a loaf of bread shaped like a pig and called the Yule Boar. It is often made from the grain of the last sheaf. This boar remains on the Yule table throughout the season and is kept till spring, when it is both fed to the oxen who will plough the fields and mixed with the new seed. It is expected to bring a good harvest.[15] Almond cakes shaped like a sow often accompanied by suckling piglets are another part of Swedish Yule fare. Freya's sow aspect was known as Syr. This was also Her solar aspect. In Germany today, when the sun is very hot, they still say "Die gelbe Sau brennt," or "The yellow Sow is burning."[16] Tacitus tells us that the Mother Goddess was worshiped once by the Celtic Aestii, and that as a symbol of their religion, they carried carved figures of boars that they believed would keep them from harm.

In folklore, the story of the sun held prisoner in the tower survived as the story of the maiden with long golden hair, held prisoner by the ugly hag. It is important to remember here that both crone and maiden are aspects of the same Goddess. At the solstice, the old sun gives birth to, or releases, Her maiden self. As a maiden dressed in white, and with golden hair, bearing the light of the regenerated sun (which was also Herself), She survived almost intact as Lucia or St. Lucia. Although Lucia's worship probably began in Northern Italy, Her immediate acceptance and survival argue that She may have been seen as similar to an older indigenous form of the Goddess. Her day is December 13 in Sweden (the

29

Winter Solstice on the old calendar), and it is considered the start of Yule. In preparation for Her celebration, the house is purified, all threshing, spinning and weaving put in order, and weeks of holiday bread baking and candle making are finished. Often candles are made from pig's fat that is believed to contain the vitality of the pig. Lutsfisken (a special fish dish) is buried in ashes, to be ready for eating on Christmas. The elders tell us that the Lucia, clothed in white and crowned with light, moves at dawn across ice bound lakes and brings food for the poor.[17]

There are significant correlations here to the giant Skadi. She was once probably connected with bonfires and accompanied by torch processions as She still is in Sicily and Italy.[18] Lucia is represented in most households by the eldest daughter, who rises before dawn and is dressed in white and crowned with evergreen (or lignon leaf) and candles and wears a crimson sash. Followed by her younger sisters also dressed in white and each bearing a lighted candle, she brings her mother coffee and Lussekatter. Translated as "Lucia cats" or "light cats", they are bread seasoned with cardamom and shaped like sunwheels.[19] In Norway, She is described as a "loose woman" and said to lead the Wild Hunt. She is sometimes referred to as a "goblin."[20] Here again, we see Her association with the crone who is the other side of Herself. Christian legend says that She was a virgin, who gouged out Her eyes rather than be violated. She was held prisoner in a temple from which She could not be moved, and a fire was built around Her, but like Gollveig, it could not harm Her.[21] Like Freya or Nerthus, She heralded the season of peace and plenty.

In Scandinavia, many of the oldest aspects of the Goddess were seen as giants, like Skadi, or were the daughters of giants. The giants were divided into different types associated with the features of the earth and nature over which they were seen to have some control. They appear to represent the remains of the oldest Scandinavian deities. In Thurs we have the good one, pregnant with possibilities. She is the force of awakening and growth. The sow is Her Epiphany. Thurisaz can be used to break down boundaries, to push past whatever holds you back. Call on Her when your life needs opening to new possibilities.

4. Ansuz: Mouth

Ansuz is the source of direct communication with the Goddess. It is the rune of speech. From this rune come the divine utterances of the Goddess: all forms of words of power—spells, incantations and poetry, as well as songs. It is at once the whole of oral tradition. Before written history, all the traditions that told a people who and what they were, were contained in the stories and songs handed down from generation to generation. The word *ansuz* literally means a godling: a divine ancestor, a foremother. Later the phonetic meaning changed from a to o. The new name had the literal meaning of mouth. But the meaning of the rune itself was not changed. The wisdom of ancestors is still accessible to the tribe through ritual and magic; through them the words of the Goddess can be known. From the mouth of the Goddess comes the inspiration which can provide guidance. Inspiration means literally, to breathe in, "to infuse with an exalting or quickening influence... to guide or control by divine influence."[1] It is interesting to note that there are engravings on bone from the Mesolithic Maglemosian culture found in Zealand, Denmark, which show a figure whose body is composed of this rune. Marija Gimbutas feels such figures, made up of Her symbols, represent the Bird Goddess.[2]

Words of power are one of the sources of magic, as are the runes. So Ansuz represents the magical power of the runes to convey to us messages from the Goddess in any of Her forms. She is the source of all being. Long before patriarchal gods stole the power of naming and language, Hers was the magical power inherent in the power of song, words and spells. Christianity remembered this magic and, indeed, claimed it for its own god. The Christian text tells us: "In the beginning was the word, and the word was with God, and the word was God."[3] The Eddic Goddess Saga (whose name gives us the verb *to say*)[4] gave Her name to the sagas or songs of history. She lived in Sokvabek, a crystal hall. Sokvabek was located beneath a cool river from which Saga (and Odin) drank daily. The river was also called "the stream of time and events."[5] Thus, time and events were fluid, as was the oral tradition in which they were held. When written history came into being, it was often seen as much less accurate than an oral tradition because it became static, fixed in a particular form. Her poets preserved the history of Her people in songs, and in so doing shaped it as well. Poetry was considered sacred and a gift of divine inspiration.

There is a very strange myth in the Eddas about the source of poetic inspiration. When the old and new Eddic pantheons came to a truce, they sealed it by all spitting into a jar. From this spittle was formed a man, Kvasir, whose name comes from a word for beer. He inspired others to use their own wisdom. He was murdered, and his blood, caught in a cauldron and two jars, was mixed with honey and fermented to form a mead. Those who drank the mead acquired wisdom and poetry. This myth has several interesting points. First of these is the forming of a wise man from the waters that came from the mouth of the gods and Goddesses. The life-giving substance of the Goddess was not air but water. It was always Her bodily fluids which were the source of life. Rivers are also said to have mouths, and water as the source of life was often sacred to the Goddess (see Laguz). Second, the mead was made from blood and honey. In this case, since the source of the blood was male, he must be killed to shed it; but of course the original wise blood was menstrual blood. The third point is the association of the drinking of a fermented beverage with communication with the gods and thus the attaining of inspiration. There is evidence that the making and drinking of fermented brews (mead and beer) was a sacred act. The drinking of such beverages could provide a magical link to both ancestors and divinity.[6] This sacred mead is kept in the cave of a giantess, under a sacred mountain. Once again this reminds us that the original source of inspiration belongs to the Goddess as crone.

Ansuz, or mouth, is the Goddess as source of all speech: song, history, poetry and the magic in naming and words. She is the source of inspiration, the ways in which Her daughters create and partake in Her divinity. This is an especially important rune for artists, writers and storytellers, because it means that they are able to hear Her voice clearly. If you are using your creativity in some project, this rune is telling you your vision is true, that it comes from your deepest source. What you are working on is important, and it is your job to bring it into being. If Ansuz comes to you in a reading, listen carefully for the voice of the Goddess; She has something to say to you. Listen for Her voice within you. Use Ansuz in your spellwork both when you need to hear Her voice and when you need Her to hear you.

Ansuz is the power of all naming. Think of the many thousands of names for the Goddess. Speak your own names of power. Remember that She is the source of all being, and honor Her with all you say. Know that all history is fluid, including your own. You can rewrite the stories you tell yourself about yourself, reshape your personal mythology. Call on Her and the power of Ansuz to shape the words of your spells and incantations. Know that speech can call things into being. We cannot conceive of that which we lack the words to describe. Words can limit what we see as possible. Invent new language. Remind others of its power. Sing Her songs in your rituals. Honor and invoke Her with poetry.

5. Raidho: Wagon

Raidho is the path of the sun, the dance of the seasons, the pattern behind events, the round of life. To the Danes and Swedes, the constellation we know as Ursa Major was known as the Wagon, the literal meaning of this rune. In it the sun traveled across the night sky. An example of this Sun Wagon was found in a peat bog at Trundholm in Zealand, dating around 1000 BCE. On it rode a large gilded bronze disk of the sun.[1] The Goddess who rode the Sun Wagon was probably Nerthus. According to Tacitus (c.100 BCE), Nerthus dwelt on a sacred island in the ocean. There She lived in the heart of a grove. At a certain point each year, Her presence would enter a Sacred Wagon. She would then travel across the lands in Her wagon drawn by cows. Wherever She went there was rejoicing. All weapons were set aside and peace and prosperity followed Her. Eventually She grew tired, and returned to Her grove, where She and Her Wagon were bathed in a lake by slaves who were then drowned, for none who saw Her in Her bath could live.[2] She was represented at Her ceremonies by a naked priestess, with long hair, wearing a torc, arm and leg bracelets made of gold. In Nordic regions, She was later associated with the Goddess Frigg.[3] A small bronze Goddess with large round eyes and one hand at Her breast, clothed only in a girdle and necklace, found at Faardal in Jutland and dated at Middle Bronze Age, may be an early representation of Her. Her other hand probably held the reins of a wagon, which may have been drawn by the bronze snake found with Her.[4] In Raidho we have the Goddess as the patterner, She who shapes the cycles of life with Her own movements. One of the names by which Nerthus was known was the Dancer. Hers was the dance of life itself, the pattern of the heartbeat, the cyclical turning of Her wagon.

Much as fire is said to dance upon the hearth, the sun was said to dance in the sky, particularly on the mountain tops of Sweden, where Her footprints left marks on the stones. Petroglyphs of footprints, dating from the Bronze Age, are found next to solar wheels and boats (the forerunners of the wagon). Occasional touching footprints formed a solar wheel, as the flyfot or flying foot (swastika), one of Her oldest symbols.[5] She dances most often at sunrise and over water and it is considered lucky to see Her dance. In Germany, She dances at Easter and girls gather water at rivers (where the sun has bathed) and bathe in it to bring them beauty for the year; or gather dew at sunrise to wash their faces.[6] In Denmark, the sun is said to dance on Pinse morning (50 days after Easter). Houses are purified, new clothes put on, and in Kobenhavn "all rise at dawn and go to Frederiksberg hill, to see the sun rise and dance."[7]

Sacred dances, or rounds, were a part of the celebration of many Pagan holidays, their motion reflecting the turning of the wheel of life. The energy of human participants was a necessary part of the wheel's turning, as all life was known to be interrelated. The Greek word for dance, *dromenon*, from *drao*, meant in Ancient Greek " a ritual pattern of dynamic expression." Many times the pattern of the dance was marked out. The pattern on the floor of Chartres Cathedral is that of a labyrinth or maze dance. Such mazes, constructed of stones, are found in parts of Finland, Norway, Sweden, Denmark and Northern Germany.[8] They were often called Troytowns (*trojeborg* in Sweden) from the OHG *draja*, Celtic *troian*, meaning to turn or twist.[9] They were also called Stone Dance. Stories and customs of both Sweden and Denmark associate the circles with round dances performed in them in spring, where a young maiden representing the spring sun is danced out from the center.[10] There is a connection here as well with the spiral dance of the Craft. The word *maze* is etymologically a Scandinavian word. It referred to a "state of bewilderment or confusion." Related Swedish and Norwegian words mean "to dream" and "a languid state."[11] The maze dances were meant, in part, to create a trance state in the dancer, where one could travel "between the worlds" to that place of ritual where the circle is complete and the pattern of all life/death/rebirth is perceivable.

The dance associated with the labyrinth in Delos and on Crete was the crane dance (Greek, *geranos*). From the same root word comes the Lithuanian *garnys* or stork—both waterbirds associated with the Goddess.[12] Both birds are associated with the Goddess in Scandinavia as well. In Denmark, the return of the storks to their yearly nesting sites marks the beginning of spring. Special platforms are built for their nests on the roofs of houses, for they are thought to bring good luck. Even when the top of a chimney becomes the site of a nest, as happens not infrequently, the birds are honored and not disturbed. Likewise, spring is marked in Sweden by the return of the cranes from their winter migration. Were either of these birds associated with the Scandinavian form of the maze dance?

The Dancer of the runes is the Goddess, and Her dance is the dance of life—the great dance of which everything is a part. To be aware of this dance is to feel your connection to everything in the universe. Often we are so immersed in the act of living that we lose sight of the larger patterns in our own lives and the world. If Raidho comes to you, look for the larger picture. It is an invitation to put events in a larger perspective. Use Raidho to call on Her when you have lost sight of the pattern of energy that flows through and shapes your life. Once we are in touch with the pattern, we see the footsteps of the Goddess in Her dance all around us.

Raidho is the energy pattern underneath all life, portrayed by the passage of the sun's wagon across the sky. It can be an important rune for witches. Use it to reinforce the pattern of your spells and to bind them to work always within the natural patterns of the universe. Use Raidho to guide you into trance work. Honor Her by dancing Her rounds and celebrate Her each time you step between the worlds.

A small bronze figurine of the Goddess with huge round sun-like eyes and a hand at Her breast, wearing a necklace and girdle. She and Her snake are from the Middle Bronze Age and were found at Faardal, Jutland. (h. 2½ inches)

6. Kenaz: Torch

Kenaz means torch. The torch is a symbol of the Goddess as the Life Bringer. Several Goddesses who survived into historic times were associated with torches and torch processions. Hecate, who is shown carrying a torch, was sometimes called Phosphorus or "light bearer".[1] Torch light processions were part of the rituals of Demeter, as She searched each fall for Persephone. The changing leaves were said to take on the color of torches to light Her way. Artemis held a torch in one hand.[2] Diana Nemorensis was worshiped in Her sacred grove with "a multitude of torches," and women whose prayers She answered brought lighted torches to Her grove to fulfill their vows.[3] Likewise, Eileithyia, Goddess of childbirth, was sometimes shown holding a torch: when it was pointed up birth could proceed; carried down it meant death.[4] Her torch was the vital fire of life energy. She was associated as well with divination, snakes and the fire of the hearth. On Crete, Her home was in a sacred cave where women came for Her help in labor until the last century. Here Her image, holding a child, was carved from a living column of stone. She was called the Opener; She was not only the opener of the womb, but by extension She was the gates of life and death. Her cave was marked by an omphalos stone, the center of the earth, as She was the umbilical cord.

Hestia's fire, the fire of the hearth, was also called the center of the earth,[5] and like Eileithyia, She was the gate of life and death. She received the richest part of the sacrifices in Her celestial dwelling place.[6] The torch of the Life Bringer and the fire of the hearth are both the vital fire of the force of life. Both Hestia and Her Roman counterpart Vesta were shown with torches that represented the life force as the perpetual fire. Perpetual fires burned in Freya's temples in Sweden. The rune Kenaz relates to this same fire. It is the center of the ceremonial circle as it is of the home. Around it, the cycles of the seasons are celebrated. Many cultures recognize the sun's fire and the hearth fire as the same. Processions or races with burning torches were used to spread the beneficial influence of the sun's light. In Sweden, in what is probably a remnant of an older Pagan Winter Solstice ritual, people in rural areas start out for church on Christmas morning before the sun rises. They travel in sleighs carrying torches of evergreen boughs as they move across the fields. As they reach the church, the torches are used to form a bonfire encouraging the sun to burn as brightly when it rises.[7]

Kenaz represents the fire of life as the vital force that energizes humans, animals and crops alike. Crops were visited with torch light processions at several times during the Pagan year. In all probability, the flame's energy of warmth and light, like the sun, was brought to the land as a form of sympathetic magic. Spelled Kano, it was associated with the rituals of the Goddess Nerthus and the power of Her energy moving through the land.[8] Tacitus tells of Her cart processions (see Raidho) and the carrying of torches was probably part of the same ritual. This is the Goddess as the embodiment of the life energy, and consequently of both crop and human fertility. At or just before sowing time, the Goddess made a circuit of the fields, turning around them, and with Her energy miraculously increased the ability of the fields and seeds to produce a bountiful harvest. As part of this process, the fields were protected from all harm; thus, the continuation of human life was protected as well. In parts of Scandinavia, land was officially claimed by carrying fire around its boundaries or by shooting a fiery arrow across it.[9]

Kenaz is the life energy of the Goddess. It is the vital fire that quickens the babe in the womb, the crop in the fields, the spring season in the land. This energy is represented by the fire of the hearth or the torches carried through the fields. She guards the gates of life and death, and with proper ritual we can partake of Her magic. To draw Kenaz is to be in touch with the energy of the life force. It is a good time to ask yourself where you are putting your energy. We have the power within us to create our own reality. When you draw Kenaz, you are in touch with that power. You can call on it at will to manifest your needs and desires. Honor Her when you light candles on your altar. Strengthen your magic by marking the rune on the candles you use in your spells. Whisper its name when you sit by the fire in winter and feel the strength of Her life energy warm you. Invoke the magic of Kenaz to call on the power in Her ever-burning flame.

7. Gebo: Gift

Gebo means gift. This is the Goddess as the All-Giver. In Scandinavia, this was a title taken on by the god Odin, but it had belonged from the beginning to the Goddess. Gebo was the function of the Goddess, as the parthenogenic source of all life, to bring forth crops in abundance. She was celebrated at the time of planting. Several of the Goddesses of the Scandinavian pantheon retain traces of Her power.

One of Freya's kennings was also Gefn or All-Giver. Her name came from *gefa*, to give, as did the name of the Danish Goddess Gefjun, who was commonly known as the Goddess of the plough.[1] Like Freya, She was probably a descendant of Nerthus. Gefjun was invoked and honored at the time of sowing. In Denmark, the appearance of storks in the spring signaled the arrival of planting time, as did the return of the cranes to Sweden. In both cases, it was the time when the All-Giver would again bring the gift of new crops. Her traditional plough rites were celebrated at the New Year in both Scandinavia and England. They consisted of a plough drawn through the town and fields on a wagon, led by a woman and drawn by men masked as oxen.[2] She was also Golden Gefjun, who turned Her four sons into oxen and with them ploughed Denmark (Jutland) from Sweden. Like Frigg, Gefjun was said to know the destinies of all, for She was an aspect of the Goddess as Fate.

She was responsible for women who died unwed, and She was called on in oath taking. Like Freya, She owned a magical shining necklace obtained through the bestowing of Her sexual favors.[3]

While Gefjun's wagon was drawn by oxen, Freya's was drawn by cats—two black lynx. There is a Finnish spirit that brings money, milk, cream and butter—and takes the shape of a cat, called a Buttercat.[4] Its name comes from a Swedish word *Bjara* or *Bara*, meaning Bearer, or Giver. There is a similar Lappish version called a *Smieragatto*.[5] The cat may have been sacred to the Goddess as All-Giver. In other parts of the world, similar associations have been found. A seated Goddess giving birth, found in a grain bin at Catal Huyuk, was also accompanied by two cats. Part of the ritual celebrations of St. Lucia, who is said to bring food in winter to feed the poor, includes the eating of "lightcats" or cat cakes. These cakes are also called Golden Carriages and are made from wheat flour colored golden with saffron. Their shape is that of a sunwheel.[6] It consists of the X of the rune shape, with each end a spiral, bringing it energy and motion, a magical means of calling forth the gifts of the All-Giver. The baking of sacred breads for use in rituals, often shaped into loaves that represented the Goddess or decorated with Her symbols, has continued since the Neolithic. Loaves or pieces of bread were sometimes ritually buried in the fields at sowing time.

Gefjun's wagon rituals undoubtedly came from the older rituals of fertility and abundance attributed to Nerthus. With time, the plough itself became a sacred object. In the aspect of All-Giver, She was responsible for both human fertility and the fertility of the fields and seed. Such association of female and crop fertility was present even in medieval accounts of the rural crop sowing festivals that became attached to local folk figures.[7] In Savoy as late as the nineteenth century, a woman described as half-naked and seated on a chair in a cart was drawn through the fields.[8] At Autun, the accounts specifically referred to bawdy behavior.[9] The rituals ended with the plough being thrown into the water or being burned. Remember that the circuit of the fields made yearly by Nerthus ended with Her ritual bath of renewal, probably meant to restore Her virginity.

The Goddess Frigg has been reduced to Odin's wife and matron of marriage and weddings. Still there are remnants of the All-Giver to be found here as well. She is referred to as the Mother of all the gods. Foremost among Her maidens is Fulla, whose name means abundance. Fulla is said to distribute gifts from Frigg's coffer.[10] This magical coffer, like Pandora's box, the coffer of Aphrodite or Tanit, or Idun's coffer where She keeps the golden apples of immortality, is of course the womb of the Goddess, source of all life. Fulla is described as a maid with long golden hair, worn loose except for a band of gold about Her head.[11] Her unbraided hair is a sign of Her virginity and power. It is likened to a field of waving grain, which is one of the many gifts of the All-Giver. The snood (headband/fillet) of Fulla is a *kenning* (Eddic metaphor) for gold.[12] Fulla is also in charge of Frigg's shoes (a symbol for female sexuality) and knows Her secret plans (as an aspect of fate).[13]

Gebo is the gifts of the Goddess. Use the rune when you are beginning a new project on which you would invoke Her blessings. She brings forth all Her gifts from within Herself and we honor Her when we too use our inner power to create and bring forth. Call on Gebo to help you recognize and actualize your own gifts. Recognize the gift of Her life force in the food you eat. All gifts are an exchange of energy. Be conscious of both what you receive and what you give.

8. Wunjo: Joy

Wunjo means joy or bliss. The Britannica World Language Dictionary defines heaven as "a state of bliss, extreme happiness."[1] Even into Christianity, the Pagan concept of the world after death as a place of great joy has clearly survived. In Scandinavia, it was Hel's domain, the holy land of the underworld. The dead were believed to "die into the hill."[2] After death they continued to live, in the hollow places under the mountains or hills or in the barrows. These underworld halls were places filled with light where the dead ate and drank and gave their attention to the well being of their kin or clan in the world of the living. Barrows were usually located near dwellings so that dead ancestors could watch over the living and the living could honor the dead. It was believed that too much mourning or sorrow by those who remained would bring pain or harm to the dead. Instead they were offered sacrifices and sometimes worshiped. The dead were not cut off from the living. They could attend their own funerals and might even be visible to the living. They could rejoin their loved ones in the world above for short periods of time. At Jul, the gates between the worlds were open and the dead could attend feasts laid in their honor. At other times, people might come across a barrow lying open and filled with light. The dead might speak and appeared happy. They cared about the welfare of their descendants and might offer advice. People might go to an ancestral barrow to obtain information about the future. Sometimes a particular ancestor was seen as inhabiting a special stone. They could communicate with the living through dreams as well.[3] These beliefs reflect a world view where death was seen as a stage in the vast web of life/death/rebirth. It was not feared as final or separate from life. As the Goddess went under the hill in the fall to reemerge in spring, so too the dead passed under the hill. There they lived well and joyously. While they dwelled in their underworld forever, their spirits could also be reborn to the tribe.

As Christianity found a hold in Scandinavia, Hel's domain changed. It became a place not of joy but of sorrow. Still, its descriptions can tell us something of its original form. It was a bitterly cold land. Its forests were deep and pathless. It glittered. It was surrounded by or gave off great light. This was a description of winter and the ice and snow that covered the earth in Scandinavia, particularly in the northern regions.

It was also surprisingly consistent with the Pagan Otherworld as it was most often described in the literature of the Middle Ages. The sanctuary of the Mother was usually described as an island, orchard, or garden that lay across the sea, under the water, or under the hill or mountain. Here a Queen ruled. She dwelled in a "chamber of crystal."[4] Here "all the rays of the sun converge" giving "a striking impression of light, that seems to rise from the very landscape."[5] The Queen Herself had hair as gold as the sun, and sometimes Her name meant sun as well.[6] The hero, or Her lover by medieval times, was "recreated by the rays from Her eyes."[7] In the romances of the time, She was known as the "dispenser of joy."[8]

The winter sun went under the hill, or into the womb cave, to be reborn in spring. But at the same time, it traveled over the water into darkness and reappeared each morning, except at the depths of winter. Then it sat for a long time on the horizon, finally sliding into the sea, where it remained through days of darkness. Both myths had an effect on the Scandinavian underworld. The Old English word *glaed* meant both joy and shining, brightness.[9] At sunset, the sun was said to "gladden" or "glitter with joy." One of the Eddic kennings for gold and names for Freya was Mardoll, "shining over the sea."[10] The reflection of the sun on the water sometimes caused the appearance of a circular island that lay to the west.[11] The Irish called it Tier-na-Og. Their concept of an island where the dead dwelled once again young, well and without death probably influenced Scandinavian mythology.

The Eddic concept of the afterlife placed the Otherworld in the plane of the gods. By the time of Sturluson, Hel's domain was equated with misery and was only for those who died of disease or in bed. Those who died bravely in battle hoped to be chosen by Freya or Odin to dwell in their halls, as maidens go to Gefjun and the drowned to Ran. But the stories are far from consistent on many points. The influence of Christianity can be seen in the change that dictated the manner in which one died, and the purity of one's heart decided where one would end up. The Viking concept of Odin's Valhalla was one where warriors feasted and fought throughout time, awaiting the final battle at the end of the world. But early barrow graves do not show weapons as grave goods. Valhalla lay near to Gladsheim, hall of gladness, where the Eddic pantheon gathered in council.[12] Or it "stands gold-bright and wide in Gladsheim, Abode of joy, a heavenly place."[13] It lay in the shimmering grove of Glaesir, where the leaves of the trees were made of red gold.[14] But its description is not very different from Hel's domain. It is still the same Otherworld in many respects. And even the Eddas are inconsistent as to who goes where. The late Eddic god Baldur, when killed, went to Hel's underworld. Eddic funerals were journeys by ship across the sea as the sun traveled. The ships were set afire and sent off towards the horizon.

The Danish barrow dead were later called elves or fallen angels. In Sweden, it was the Alvor, descendants of the Eddic Alfar, who dwelt in the mounds. These folk, with fairylike habits, came out from their mounds to dance in circle dances. There is a runic inscription on a stone at Lagno that refers to the Alfar. It shows an elf with raised arms clasping two snakes.[15] The snake was the constant companion of the Goddess of the Otherworld, no matter how much it changed. Her domain might be described as filled with snakes, or She might use them to bridle the wolf She rode.

46

This stone, showing an elf or Goddess with Her two snakes, is at Lagno, Sweden, and dates from c. *400* CE.

Two snakes were said to feed on the roots of the world tree. The ancestral dead were said to be able to take snake form. In such form, they appeared to children, protecting them from harm and telling them secrets. The snake was often believed to guard some great treasure.[16] The snake was also associated with ships, from the earliest rock carvings, through the Snake Goddess and Her ship found at Faardal in Denmark (see Raidho) to the Viking burials on dragonships, with snakelike prows. In obvious imitation of the Goddess, Odin was said to take snake form.

Wunjo is the rune of the Otherworld, the land of joy, the Domain of the Queen of the Dead and Her snakes. Hel is one of Her surviving aspects, as is Freya. Call on Her snakes to guard you and share their secrets with you. Know that the treasure they guard is the journey to rebirth. Invoke Her when you would speak with the dead. Remember to honor your foremothers and ask them to work on your behalf. Use Wunjo in your spellwork to help you lay aside the stress of day-to-day things and taste the joy of the Other-world, a joy not found separate from life, but in the fullness of it.

9. Hagalaz: Hail

Hagalaz means hail. It is the rune of the Goddess as the Destroyer; the hail that could kill or damage crops and livestock; the Storm Bringer. The power to bring storms was assigned to several of the late Scandinavian survivals of the Great Goddess. The Valkyries brought not only dew but also hail. The Finnish Goddess Thorgerd, who was later called a troll, used magic to aid those who invoked Her and caused thunder, lightning and hail when She came to their aid.[1] Splintered into many pieces, the Storm Bringer survives in folklore and customs as the witch, the troll, the demon. She appears as a crooked old woman, with the beaked nose of the hag (and the bird Goddess). Her time is the Winter Solstice during the celebration of Yule, when the spirits of the dead are said to be able to return to the lands where they had lived. She is Kari tretten or Kari the thirteenth, the troll woman racing over the countryside on the thirteenth of January as the Norwegians ride in sleighs and sledges over the frozen lakes and roads ringing bells to drive away the Christmas.[2] She is the ugly figure of straw that Swedish boys make on January thirteenth and put in front of the houses of girls who have rejected them as suitors.[3] In Upper Bavaria, She is still said to wander around the fields and harm people and animals during the twelve days of Christmas.[4] On January sixth, people don ugly wooden masks that are handed down from generation to generation. They have fangs, bulging eyes, wrinkles and disarrayed hair. Carrying brooms, chains and hatchets, they crack long whips and drive out Frau Perchta, Goddess of the dead. She and Her cohorts are then said to "fructify the fields and frighten naughty children."[5]

Her power lies in Her hair. With it She can cause storms. Through its combing and binding or unbinding, it could cause destruction. As late as the seventeenth century witches were accused of causing wind, hail and lightning with their hair.[6] But Her hair is also Her regenerative energy and the energy of the sun's rays; as such, it is often described as long and golden. It is the hair of gold made in the forge of the dwarfs for Freya in Her aspect as Sif. In Germany, special breads were baked for Winter Solstice and offered as sacrifices to Holla as Mother of the Dead. The loaves were called Holla's braid or Hollenzopf.[7] The loaves themselves were braided, probably to bind the power in Her hair.

Similar loaves are baked in many parts of Europe around the Spring Equinox when the storms of winter have to be turned aside to allow the spring renewal. Sometimes whole eggs are baked into the openings between braids. In Sweden on Holy Thursday, witches are said to ride brooms to Blakulla mountain. There they stir cauldrons, and concoct evil spells.[8] Farmers protect their farms from the Easter witch by marking tar crosses over doors and keeping their ploughs locked up. There are bonfires on the hill tops.[9] In Denmark on May Eve (Valborgsaften in Jutland), witches are said to fly to meet the devil at the Brocken. Bonfires are lit to bring protection from evil spirits abroad in the land.[10] She tops the bonfire on Midsummer's Eve as the witch or winter hag, and songs are sung of the conquest of darkness.[11] In Germany, Her effigy as winter is burned on Shrove Tuesday to celebrate the fact of Her defeat by Dame Sun.[12]

According to Thorsson, another meaning still associated with this rune is the rime egg or ice egg of Scandinavian creation.[13] The rime egg symbolizes both creation and the seasonal recreation of spring from winter's cold bonds. Even today, most of us recognize the egg as a symbol of the returning sun and the energy of new growth. We may associate it with the Easter egg but like many symbols, the Easter egg is a symbol of far older Pagan spring rituals of renewal. In Germany, eggs laid on Green Thursday (the Thursday before Easter) are said to stay fresh all year.[14] Eggs ploughed into the fields at this time are supposed to bring a plentiful harvest, and one kept in the house is said to protect the house and its occupants from lightning all year long.[15] It is traditional for eggs to be brought to children by the fox, stork or cuckoo rather than by the Hare.[16] Eggs are dyed and decorated with traditional designs passed down through generations from mother to daughter and given to family and friends. The oldest unbroken tradition of egg decorating comes from the Ukraine, where it goes back 10,000 years.[17] Here the "most ancient and significant motifs" are symbols of the sun, which is seen as the "all embracing, all renewing, all birth giving force"[18] of the Goddess. Almost every *pysanka* (traditional decorated egg), ancient or new, uses one or more symbols of the sun. These include the "circle, swastika, tripod, and star or rose."[19] In Bavaria on Palm Sunday, branches of trees are bent into semicircles (split eggs) attached to poles, decorated with gaudy glass beads which catch the sunlight and set in the fields. They are believed to bring fertility to the crops and to offer protection from hail and drought.[20]

Hagalaz is a rune of protection as well as of death and storms. It is the full force of the Goddess as Destroyer, Protector and Creatrix, each in its proper season. She is responsible for keeping the natural world in harmonious balance. The ninth rune, it is called the Mother rune.[21] Its six spokes are the magic of three doubled, of increase. Its sacred number nine is both the triple, Triple Goddess and the period of gestation. In Egypt, this same shape was called the *double furka*.[22] Its meaning was "a full season composed of two halves," and it "represented the unity of the natural world."[23] The six-spoked wheel was said to "radiate strength."[24]

Use Hagalaz to bring the harmony that comes when things are seen in perspective. Let it remind you of the necessary place of the Destroyer in the cycle of life. Have you stood in a thunderstorm, watching the thunder and lightning and felt awed by its strength and destructive power? This is the vital force of the Goddess moving through nature. Use Hagalaz to invoke its strength and its protection. In Hagalaz the Goddess is wild and untamed, moving in a world over which humans have no control. When we began to see ourselves as the center of the universe, this power and She who wielded it were called evil. Out of fear of this aspect of the Goddess and Her women who could call on Her magic, much harm has been done both to women and to the earth. Invoke Hagalaz with care and respect.

10. Naudhiz: Need-Fire

Naudhiz, or need-fire, is a fire started at times of hardship or disaster. Human participation in Her mysteries was necessary to the proper functioning of the universe. When disaster struck, proper use of those mysteries could restore the harmony of Her order. Need-fires were started by friction—either the rubbing together of two pieces of wood or with a pole and a wheel. The use of friction to start the need-fire was also seen as sexual, representing the heat of passion. Thus, it was also said that a need-fire could be started from a woman's genitals.[1] The heat of human sexuality was not separate from the heat of the need-fire or the heat of the sun bringing new life and rebirth to the land in season. The need-fire was a means of petitioning the Goddess for a renewal of the fires of life. A need-fire could be used to protect people or animals and to ward off disease. Cattle or other livestock were driven through the smoke, or between two need-fires. Sometimes, in order for the magic of the need-fire to be effective, it was necessary to extinguish all other fires first. Hearth fires were later relit with a brand from the sacred fire.

It is likely that most, if not all, of the Pagan fire festivals were started with need-fires. Certainly there is evidence that both the Imbolc and Midsummer's Eve fires were begun this way.[2] In some areas, the fires of Midsummer were started by lighting a wagon wheel, plaited with straw and attached to the top of a tall pole.

The wheel served to represent the sun at the top of the world tree. In Sweden, maypoles constructed for the Midsummer's Eve festivities still take the same shape—tall poles with one or more plaited circles at the top, often of birch, decorated with flowers and ribbons. Throughout many parts of Europe as late as the nineteenth century, the custom survived of throwing burning wheels into the air or rolling them down hills at Midsummer. The turning wheels represented the sun turning in its own journey across the sky. Bonfires were lit on hill tops and along the coasts.

In Sweden, Denmark and Norway, most of the population still leaves the cities at Midsummer, the time in the far north of the midnight sun. They go to the forests, water or fields where huge bonfires are kindled. Birch branches, a sign of rebirth (see Berkano), are found everywhere from doorways to truck grilles.[3] The direction that the flames of the Midsummer bonfire are blown by the wind foretells the warmth or cold of the season ahead.[4] What is now a means of prediction was undoubtedly once a form of sympathetic magic. The Jul fires were also need-fires, designed to strengthen the sun as it reached the northernmost point in its course, and to insure its return. Like the returning sun or human sexuality, the flames of the need-fires called forth life. Fire was the means by which disaster and disease could be transformed. The ashes from such fires were a potent charm bringing fertility to the fields or protection from harm.

Save the ashes from your sacred holiday fires to use in spellwork throughout the year. Make a pouch to hold them, marked with the rune. Hang it in your home or car for protection.

Naudhiz comes from a place of distress, sometimes of pain. But it represents a solution as well. It is the power of the will, an essential tool in performing magic, to call into manifestation that which is needed. With it comes the vital energy of the powers of the South, the powers of fire. Here are desire, passion, the power to create. You can bring about that which you want in your life. Naudhiz reminds you that Her spark is within you. Feel the fires of life burning in the cells of your body. Know that by using your will, you can create magic. Naudhiz is outside the calendar. You can draw it to you at any point in the cycle when you feel threatened or think you need help to escape the pain or conflict or confusion in which you find yourself. If you have drawn Naudhiz, you are ready to bring a change into your life. This is major, self-initiated change. Like the Tower or Kali card of the Tarot, this is change you choose to call forth.

In a death oriented culture, Naudhiz serves to remind us that there is another way. In Her universe, each of us must play our part in continually calling forth the life force. Each time you light a candle or a bonfire, you participate in Her miraculous powers of transformation.

11. Isa: Ice

In the far north, ice is a strong presence. Cold and ice keep the frozen fields prisoner throughout the long winter, making them impossible to till. Then, in turn, they melt to provide life-giving water for the crops. The rune Isa represents the Goddess of winter and death. In true Pagan form, this also means She is fundamental to the rebirth of the land in spring. Isa is the White Goddess of Death spread across the land. What do we know of this aspect of the Goddess?

At the time of the Eddas, ice was the domain of the rime or frost giants, as was "snow, cold, stone and subterranean fire."[1] But it was also the domain of the Goddess Skadi, whose father was a frost giant. We know very little about Skadi. She may have been of Finnish origin, but She became part of the Scandinavian pantheon and gave Her name to the region. Her companions were poisonous snakes and wolves. From the Eddic myth of the binding of Loki, we know that She set a serpent over his head to steadily drip venom onto him. He was bound in a cave and his struggles caused the earth to shake.

Like most remnants of older Goddesses, She was married to the new gods. In Skadi's case, several times. She was married to Uller and to Niord. Uller was a year god of vegetation who split the ruling of the year with Odin. His portion was the time of death and winter. His hall was called Yew-hall and he used its death wood to fashion bows. He traveled in a magical fashion on snow shoes made of bone and enchanted with runes, to turn them into a ship that traveled on land or water. Sometimes he led the Wild Hunt.[2] His attributes were clearly those of the Death Goddess and probably originally belonged to Skadi. They may have originally been twin gods or he may once have been Her consort, a god of the dying vegetation. It was said that Uller used the ice to protect the land from harm in the winter. People went to his temples to ask for a thick covering of snow in winter to make the land more fertile in spring. A good layer of snow and ice was thought to insure a good harvest.[3] In fact, everything associated with Uller is also said of Skadi, who became known as the snowshoe Goddess.

Skadi's first husband was Niord. When Her father was killed, She declared war on the gods. She was appeased by being given Her choice among them of a bridegroom. She had to choose by looking only at their feet. She attempted to pick Balder, who was closely identified with Uller. (Both were gods of light, in Uller's case the aurora borealis, and both spent time each year in Hel's domain.)[4] Instead She chose Niord, god of summer, dividing the year between their abodes. But they were incompatible and later She married Uller.

The origin of Skadi's name is not agreed upon. She may be related to the Lapp Goddess Scatach, "the woman who strikes fear." Etymologically Her name may come from the Old Norse *skadi,* harm, or from the Old English *sceadu,* shadow.[5] Like most death Goddesses, She was associated with war and sexuality. One of Skadi's sacred animals was the wolf. The wolf was seen as a scavenger and devourer; it ate the bodies of the dead, reducing them to bones—a necessary part of the process of death and rebirth. It was said of the Valkyries that when they appeared at a battle, both the raven and the wolf ate well.[6] Wolves were associated with other similar Goddesses and giants. Hel set Her wolf-dog on the corpses from which She took the souls. Unlike the Christian hell, her domain was also one of ice and cold. Hel's mother, the giant Angr-boda was also the mother of the Fenris wolf, the ultimate Eddic symbol of destruction. Angr-boda lived in the Iron Wood, where she fed three wolves. One of these was Skoll, the wolf that chased the sun and would devour it in Angr-boda's Wood at the end of the world. A kenning for the sun is "the fish of the wolf."[7]

Clearly we are looking at the symbols of continuous death and rebirth. Some scholars say that Angr-boda and Skadi, both giants, were related. In all likelihood, they were both surviving remnants of an older Death Goddess. At least one other giant shares their attributes. In the myth of the funeral of Balder, the gods were unable to push his funeral ship hard enough to give it to the sea. They were forced to call on a giant for help. Hyrrokin appeared riding on a wolf, using a bridle of venomous snakes. She gave the barge to the sea with one great, earth shaking-shove. One kenning for wolf is "horse of the giantess."[8] In Viking times, there were tales of berserkers—warriors in wolf skins who fought with a more than human energy and rage. They, too, may have originally been servants of the Death Goddess.

In descriptions of the world beyond death, folktales speak of the glass isle or glass mountain. Here a Queen reigns who dwells in a glass hall, where the sun shines brightly.[9] Once again we are reminded of the realm of ice. Isa is also identified with a bridge between the worlds, perhaps at least in part from the shape of the rune.[10] The bridge over the river Gioll into Hel's domain is described as being a bridge of crystal or glass.[11] The most famous bridge between worlds at the time of the Eddas was Bifrost, the bridge between earth and the land of the gods. It could also be seen as a bridge between death and immortality. Here, too, we have primarily a winter occurrence, for Bifrost is not the rainbow of the southern lands, but the fogbow.

Although She has been splintered into many parts, we can still recognize in Skadi the crone, death, winter aspect of a Great Goddess of life/death/rebirth. Ice then, is Her gift to the land. It brings the death of winter to the land; but it also brings the promise of renewed fertility and rebirth in the spring. This is an aspect of the Goddess our society has largely forgotten—the benevolent face of the Death Goddess. Isa can be a rune of great beauty. Think of the sunlight glittering off an unbroken sheet of ice. If you draw Isa, this may not be the time to move forward across the ice, but rather a time to wait for what is yet to come. It is a time to turn inward and find your own resources. If you engage in winter sports, use Isa in your spellwork and call on Skadi to bring you Her ice and snow. Honor Her presence in the glittering beauty of winter.

12. Jera: Harvest

The literal meaning of this rune is year or season: the physical manifestation of the turning of the sunwheel. It represents the harvest aspect of the Goddess, the fruitful season. The Goddess is omnipresent and at harvest time She is seen as being in the harvest itself. Most of the customs associated with the harvest reflect this presence. She was often called by the name of the crop; thus in Norway, children were warned not to go into the pea crop as they might be caught by the Pea Mother, who could be found sitting in the field.[1] Most often, the energy of the Goddess was believed to move through a crop ahead of the harvesters and to be gathered in the last sheaf cut. According to Frazer, in Denmark the last sheaf of rye or barley was called the Old Rye (or Barley) Mother and was larger in size. Sometimes the person who bound this sheaf was also called by the same name.[2] The last sheaf of the wheat crop was shaped to look like a woman, dressed in clothes and carried home on the wagon.[3] Depending on the area and the crop, the honoring of Her spirit might take place on the threshing floor. In Sweden, a woman was adorned with stalks of corn, crowned with its ears and then honored as the Corn Woman.[4]

Scandinavians still practice rituals connected with this last sheaf. In Sweden, the last sheaf is still believed to contain all the vitality of the harvest. It is made into a small figurine that is placed beside the table during the feasting at Jul and fed delicacies, or it is tied to a pole and put on the roof for the birds. If the birds eat all the grain, it is believed to promise a good harvest to come.[5] Similarly, in Denmark as part of the traditions associated with the celebrations of Julaften (Christmas Eve), a sheaf of grain is tied to a pole and put in the garden to feed the wild birds.[6] The customs associated with the Harvest Goddess are seen as a form of sympathetic magic, meant to bring about a desired result. The association with the last sheaf and birds clearly points to a remembered association between the harvest and the Bird Goddess. In eating the last sheaf, She regains Her vitality.

The bird most associated with the harvest in Scandinavia is the goose. In early November, now St. Martin's Day (November 10 or 11), torch-lit processions and the eating of roast goose are part of the festivities to thank Freya for the beginning of a season of peace and plenty, that lasts until Her feast day, Jul. There is an Old English word *sele*, meaning harvest, that comes from a still older Norse word that meant "happiness, prosperity, favorable time."[7] This is the bounty of Jera. It was probably associated with the journey of Nerthus across the countryside before it was attributed to Freya. Goose eaten at this time in Sweden is traditionally accompanied by stuffed apples and blood soup.[8] In Denmark, crops must be gathered by St. Martin's Day and all goose fat rendered. The roast goose eaten at this time is believed to bring a good year both to people and animals. In most parts of Scandinavia, roast goose is one of the traditional Jul foods as well. Freya is sometimes shown riding on a goose, like Aphrodite and Mother Goose. It is interesting to note that the laughter of the hag or witch is called a cackle, the word used for the noise made by geese.

The proto-Germanic name for this rune was Jera.[9] In the Louvre, there is a small Bronze Age Goddess figurine. She is identified as a Sun Goddess and Her name is Jera. Her body is shaped like a comb or fringed skirt representing energy, Her head is round, and She wears a girdle decorated with XX's. Her shape is made up largely of Her various symbols. Several examples of similarly composed Goddesses can be found in the art of the Maglemose culture of Denmark.[10] In each case, the shapes of the runes make up Her body. The symbol for Jera, both in the Elder Futhark and in alternate forms, suggests motion, fitting well with the rune's meaning. It seems to suggest a whirling or turning, as in the turning of the year and its seasons. In the Ukraine, there are dancing figures of the Goddess whose bodies are shaped like hourglasses and whose skirts are fringed and resemble combs.[11] They are very similar to the Bronze Age Jera. These Goddesses have one hand above their heads and one down,[12] in a gesture surprisingly similar to the whirling shape of the rune. In a Sardinian version, the round head similar to Jera's is surrounded by sun rays.[13] In Ireland, wheat or reeds and rushes, pulled ceremonially from the streams and rivers, are used to fashion an image known as Brigid's cross, a whirling symbol much like the rune, which protects the household and brings it luck. On a recent trip, I saw over seven regional variations of this symbol still being made.

Use the rune Jera in your spellwork to invoke Her favor on what you would harvest. Call Her forth with your laughter. When you draw Jera in your readings, consider it as a blessing on the work you have begun. Remember to acknowledge and honor Her presence in all that you harvest. Look for Her geese in the fall sky. Celebrate Her season with happiness and peace.

13. Eihwaz: Yew

Eihwaz is the yew tree. It is sacred to the Goddess in Her role as bringer of death. But death was not considered the end in Pagan times; rather, it was seen as a necessary part of the cycle of rebirth. The Goddess brought death that new life might come from it. Birth and death were not opposites, but complements, neither of which could have existed without the other. The yew tree connected the magic of life and death by completing the cycle. Yew wood makes a good fire and is extremely strong and resistant to rotting. Both the juice and seeds of the yew are poisonous, reinforcing its association with death. Yew juice is an herbal remedy for some forms of snake bite. Yew wood was used to make bows because it was a strong, durable wood and because the death magic of the tree increased the bows' accuracy. The yew, and hence Eihwaz, became associated in this way with endurance and protection. Yew trees are exceptionally long-lived—they can live for as long as 2,000 years and are evergreen.[1] The branches of the yew send down stems which become new roots. Eventually the center of the tree dies out; but the old tree and its new shoots become virtually indistinguishable.[2] Yew trees are often found in cemeteries. Folklore said that the yew sent roots into the mouths of the dead buried around them bringing them rebirth.[3] In this way, yews were believed to protect the dead and also keep them from haunting the living.[4]

The most famous tree of the Eddas was Yggdrasill, whose roots were in Hel's domain and whose trunk connected all the worlds. A golden cock usually thought to represent the sun sat at its top. Yggdrasill is usually translated as, "the horse of the terrible one." Shamanic journeys are often equated in both Scandinavia and Siberia with journeys up or down a pole/ladder or tree, referred to as the shaman's horse. While Yggdrasill is usually seen as a variety of ash tree, it has much in common with the yew. The yew tree has needle-like evergreen leaves that may have given it the name "needle ash." Some scholars believe it to be the same tree. Yggdrasill was also known as the gallows tree.

Yews are connected both to concepts of human death and immortality, and to the death and rebirth of the sun at Winter Solstice. In the Irish tree alphabet, the yew tree represented the day of the Winter Solstice.[5] Scandinavian rock art includes trees with sun wheels and wagons, ships, elk, swans, dancers and snakes. Often the trees are riding on the ships and in some images the sun is at the top of the tree. In Scandinavia, ships were often connected with funerals and death journeys. The association of the rebirth of the sun at Winter Solstice with human continuity, and the use of some form of evergreen tree as a symbol of this death and renewal, can be seen in Pagan customs that survived Christianity and lasted well into this century. In Sweden, Pagan customs at Winter Solstice included decorating homes with branches of evergreen ash or "may twigs." (*May* comes from an old Swedish word meaning to decorate with leaves and branches, not a reference to the month.)[6] On the eve of the Solstice and later on Christmas Eve, lights were left burning throughout the night to encourage the rebirth of the sun. Each farm had its own ancestral tree or *vardtrad* that was given a gift on this night. It was thought wise to give a gift to the vardtrad or ancestral tree because its fortune was seen as tied to that of the farm.[7] Old trees are still often considered sacred and venerated in special ways. The evergreen tree later became a part of Christian holidays as the Yule tree or Christmas tree around which there are circle dances. Traditional Swedish Yule celebrations include a branched candlestick, a symbol of the world tree, with the sun at its top marked by the candle flame or by a carved or painted golden bird.[8]

Two types of folktales in particular make use of the yew's Pagan associations. In one of these, the sun that sits atop the world tree is an enchanted princess (or golden bird) that must be rescued. The rescuing of the princess is through a series of trials where she takes different forms (see Uruz). The journey becomes a form of shamanic death and rebirth. In the other type of tale, a tree grows from a mother's grave so that the mother may go on helping her daughter after death. (Sometimes the birch is substituted for the yew, as in the northern European version of Cinderella.)

Yew was often carved into both runestaves and calendar sticks called rimstocks. The earliest rimstocks were medieval, but they showed the Pagan holidays. They continued in use in rural Sweden throughout the 1800s.[9]

Sacred to the Death Goddess, Eihwaz represents a letting go, a necessary ending or release so that change may come. Use Eihwaz as a symbol in your spellwork to help you in the process of cutting away that which stands in the way of life. Nothing lasts forever except when allowed to take new form. Honor Her part in the acts of creation and healing. Invoke Her with care. Remember that death has a place in the circle of life/death/rebirth. Let Eihwaz lend you strength and endurance. Use the wood of the yew tree wisely and with clear intent.

14. Perthro: Lots

Perthro is a cup for throwing lots.[1] As Fehu is the power to divine, Perthro is the act of divination, of determining one's lot in life. In Scandinavia, one's fate was determined by the three Norns. Their names (Urd, Verdandi, Skuld) are probably late additions, but the meaning behind them, "I am all that was, is and shall be," is ancient.[2] The Norns' primary job was to weave the threads of fate. Each life was a thread in the vast tapestry They wove, but it was not given to any to see the whole picture until death. This trinity remained autonomous; they were never ruled by the gods. They were called three sisters and said to have descended from a giant,[3] probably a sign of their antiquity. They were sometimes portrayed riding on wolves (called the hounds of the Norns)[4] or boars. They used a bridle of snakes (see Thurisaz). The Norns were seen as a personification of time.[5] Marija Gimbutas describes the association of snakes with the marking of time in lunar cycles. The turns or windings of the snake's body indicate counting units. A Mesolithic antler ax found at Jordlosse, Denmark, is marked with both winding snakes and an anthropomorphized serpent, showing units of 14 and 17 days.[6]

One of the duties of the Norns was to find mothers whose wombs would bring about the reincarnation of the spirits of the ancestors. They appeared at the birth of each child and set the pattern of its fate. In Finno-Ugaric tradition, when the Norns gave their blessing to a child, they put white marks on its fingernails at birth.[7] The Norns survived in folktales as fairies and witches who appeared at births and brought gifts or curses to the newborn. Linguistically, the Old Norse word *ludr*, meaning boat, also meant coffin and cradle: the uterine ark that made the journey to the underworld and was also the means of rebirth.[8] Think of the funerals during Viking times when the dead were placed on ships, set on fire and set adrift. The Teutonic word *schiff*, from which the word ship comes, has as its root the Old Norse word *skop*. It means both fate and genitals.[9] The ship was a symbol for Frigg, whose own name became slang for sexual intercourse.

During the late Middle Ages, ships were drawn on carts through Flemish towns by the Weaver's Guild around the Spring Equinox and accompanied by much "sexually explicit" behavior.[10] In Denmark, at seaport towns, boats are still drawn through town on wagons at Fastelavn (the Monday before Ash Wednesday). The drive is accompanied by horn players and dancers and makes frequent stops. The watching crowds shout "the ship is coming."[11] What ship? Probably the ship that brought the spring sun back from darkness and represented the earth's seasonal rebirth as well as the human transit. Pictures of this ship can be found in Scandinavian rock art of the second millennium BCE. They often appear with deer/elk, swans, trees, spindles, cupmarks, sunwheels and dancers[12]—all precursors of the runes, and all part of the intricate story and rituals of the Great Goddess. Other Fastelavn rituals include birching (see Berkano) and the eating of hot cross buns (marked with sunwheels), both means of taking in the strength and vitality of new life.[13] An old Danish game played at Fastelavn is called "Sla Katten af Tonden," or "knocking the cat out of the barrel." The object is to break the hanging barrel decorated with flowers. The one who does so is Cat King.[14] Remembering that cats have long been associated with the sun, and that it is two cats who pull Freya's wagon, the allegory is clear.

Although humans could not see the overall pattern, the Norns could give guidance through dreams. The Norns were invoked before casting the runes.[15] The Scandinavians saw the runes as a means of divining what could be known of the Norns' mysteries. The power of divination belonged only to women in the Northern countries. They were called prophets or Volvas.[16] The description of a runecaster in the late thirteenth century Saga of Erik the Red tells us that her hood, shoes and mittens were of white catskin.[17]

Call on the Norns when you would cast the runes and know the patterns to come. Remember that future patterns are created by both your past actions and your internal make-up—the way you respond to things. Like the Snake Goddess, when the time is right, we can slough off our old skins. Perthro also reminds us that neither the past nor the future are closed to us. Time is a continuum through which we pass, and the Goddess is the gateway through which we enter and leave. Use Perthro to deal with the finite. Call on this aspect of the Goddess to help you find your path. Honor the Norns at any new birth, and ask their blessings.

15. Elhaz: Elk

Elhaz is the elk. It may also be the swan.[1] Both appear in Scandinavian rock art along with ships, trees, sunwheels, spindles and snakes. It is easy to see the horns of the elk or the shape of the swan or other waterbird in the shape of the rune as well. There are also human forms with upraised arms found in the rock art that resemble the form of the rune. Anyone who has ever invoked the Goddess will recognize the pose as one of supplication. Through Elhaz, we invoke the Goddess as a source of protection and of the continuity of the life force. The continuity of life for a tribal community depended on the survival and growth of the food supply. Among the Finns and Lapps, this meant the well-being of the reindeer herd.

To the Norwegian Lapps, the reindeer was the sacred animal of the Sun Virgin. She was asked to bring good luck to the reindeer herds as part of Her Midsummer rituals. Reindeer sacrificed to Her were always female and when possible, white. A "sun ring" of leaves or grass was made to honor Her, and a special meal of "sun porridge" was eaten.[2] Female reindeer were antlered and the pack was led by an old female. The size of her antlers was a mark of her wisdom and ability to lead and protect the herd.

The Finns called the constellation we call Ursa Major the Great Stag.[3] Markale suggests in *Women of the Celts* that the deer may have been the sacred animal of the Arctic, and that the Epiphany of the Goddess as deer spread south during the Ice Age.[4] A divinity with deer antlers and a neck torc appears on cave walls (Siberia) from the Upper Paleolithic.[5] Fragments of a copper vessel, dated 4000–3000 BCE, found in Las Carolinas, Spain, show deer under a rayed sun, with antlers and bodies that also appear to be rayed.[6] They represent Her life giving regenerative energy. A bronze wagon, found in Stettwig, Austria, but of Greek smithing, shows the Goddess standing at its center. She is naked except for a girdle and holds aloft the round disk of the sun. Antlered deer guard either end of the wagon. It dates from the seventh century BCE.[7] Deer masked dancers were part of the New Year festivities in both Germany and England into the Middle Ages.[8] Deer were often sacred to Her in Her form most associated with the forest's heart, the trees and sacred groves (Artemis, Diana Nemetona, Nemesis). In the far north, the reindeer feed on the moss that grows in the birch forests. She survived in fairy tales as well, where women often became deer. The elk or reindeer was sacred to the Goddess in Her aspects of renewal and regeneration that maintained the continuity of the life force. She gave life to the tribe.

Renewal and regeneration were also represented by the seasonal return of waterbirds, such as the swan, from southern migration. The swan was still a symbol even in the time of the Eddas. According to the Eddas, all swans were descended from a pair of swans that fed in a well that the Norns tended at the roots of Yggdrasill. In Germany, they were considered birds of prophecy.

The Valkyries were associated with the myths of the swan maidens, whose tales exist across not only Scandinavia, but also in many other parts of the world. Swan maidens made trips to earth as swans. They would sometimes throw off their swan cloaks (or wings, crowns or neck chains) and become maidens, to bathe in secluded streams. A man who could take their swan feathers could force them to remain and to accept him as a mate until such time as they recovered the missing objects and regained their shapes as swans. This often took a period of seven years. Medieval literature often portrayed deer in a similar fashion: white, wearing a golden neck chain and able to take the shape of a maiden.[9]

This silver-gilt pendant, showing a Valkyrie with a horn, was a Swedish grave offering from the sixth century CE.

In the story of Brunhild, the most well known of the swan maidens of Eddic legend, we find both solar imagery and the dispensing of wisdom. She flew to earth in swan plumage, along with eight of her sisters. She was imprisoned by Odin in a castle which gave off great light and was surrounded by a high wall of flames. The hero who freed her from her magically induced sleep received from her the knowledge of the runes.

The Valkyries were pictured as maidens "with dazzling white arms and flowing golden hair."[10] They wore helmets and rode white steeds. Sometimes they were said to be the personification of the clouds and lightning.[11] They chose among the slain of the battlefields, and were cup bearers in Valhalla. In folk belief, the Valkyries were thought to bring both the hoar frost and the dew, and "the people ascribed to their beneficent influence much of the fruitfulness of the earth, the sweetness of the dale and mountain-slope, the glory of the pines, and the nourishment of the meadow land."[12] They were bringers of life giving waters, both insuring fertility of the land and thus the food supply, and protecting the tribe's continued existence.

Elhaz ties us to those who have gone before and to those who will come after. It is not the magic of individual rebirth, but rather the aspect of the Goddess that ensures that life itself will continue. Through Elhaz, we seek the continuity of tribe—family, friends, community. Use Elhaz to ask for Her protection. Invoke its power when you seek continuance of a special spell. When you walk in the forests and sacred groves, remember to honor this most fundamental of Her gifts. Watch for Her deer and listen well for the wisdom they may have to share with you.

16. Sowilo: Sun Goddess

Sowilo is the Sun. In Scandinavia, She was always female and an aspect of the Goddess. We may never know Her original name, but Her sunwheel can be found on Scandinavian rock art and Her solar aspects survived in several of the Goddesses who were Her descendants. All scholars seem to agree on the existence of a Bronze Age "sun cult" in Scandinavia. Linguistically, the word for sun is female in Old Norse as well as in the Germanic and Celtic languages.[1] The Eddas called Her Sunna and they still tell folktales of Her by that name in Sweden. They also tell us that among the elves She was called Fair Wheel and Alfrotheel, the Elf-beam. In Norway, She was called Sol. Both Freya and Frigg have solar characteristics.

The wheel or orb of the sun was emblematic of a cyclical view of nature and time. It was the wheel of the seasons turning, the wheel of the sun chariot, as it moved across the sky. Her journey across the dark sea of night and the even deeper darkness of winter and Her subsequent rebirth was a message of hope and renewal. She died in the darkness of winter, bringing about the death of all Nature; She was reborn in the spring, bringing about its awakening along with Her own, the birth of Her daughter, or maiden self. According to the Eddas, the Sun will die along with the rest of the pantheon at the end of the world, swallowed by the wolf that chases Her, but before She dies, She will bear one glowing daughter. Her daughter will be the Sun of the new world that follows.[2]

Human rituals were necessary to help turn Her wheel and to bring Her back when She died in the dark of winter. Here, in the far northern parts of Scandinavia, She might not appear above the horizon for as long as forty days around the Winter Solstice. In the northern regions the subsequent reappearance or rebirth of the sun was both more noticeable and of far more importance than in the Mediterranean. Across Scandinavia (Finland, Norway, Sweden and Denmark), there can be found numerous mazes constructed mostly of stone, similar to those mazes of turf found across the British isles. Folklore connected to them suggests that a young girl, representing the spring sun, waited at the center of the maze and was ceremonially danced out of it. Pat Monaghan suggests that the shape or design of these mazes may be based on the pattern the sun itself seems to make at this time of year, crisscrossing the sky just above the horizon.[3] These stone mazes were called Troytowns (Swedish, *trojeborg*). Sometimes they were referred to as Stone Dance, Giant's Fence or Giant's Castle.[4] They were places associated with the death of the winter sun, held captive (in a tower, cave, hill), and the birth and release of a new sun that would rule the new solar year. Many variations of this story appear in Scandinavian fairy tales. One variation can be found in the Eddas themselves. In this story, a giant offers to rebuild the strong circular wall that once surrounded Asgaard and demands as his price the sun, moon and the Goddess Freya. In this instance she is described in terms that heighten Her ties to the ancient Sun Goddess: Her necklace Brisingamen and the rest of Her gold jewelry shines bright, as does the garment She wears until none (but Odin) can look at Her directly. She cries golden tears. Through the gods' trickery, the wall is not completed in the time agreed on and Freya is not given to the giant.[5] Only in winter could the sun be kept from shining.

The Sun Virgin appears on the drums of Scandinavian Lapp shamans. They offer Her sacrifices of white, female animals. In Norway, at the end of winter, doors are marked with butter that the

This sun disc of gilded bronze is from the Early Bronze Age, c.1000 BCE. It was found, together with the wagon it rode in, in a peat bog in Trundholm, Zealand.

rays of the Sun Goddess will fall on them and be fed when She first reappears. Among the Norwegian Lapps, rituals are held to honor Her at Midsummer. A sun circle is fashioned from grass or leaves, and a special porridge is eaten. In Finland, farmers pray to Her as She rises. Facing east in their fields, they say, "My dear Sun, my provider, give peace, health, look over everything, watch over everything."[6]

When Odin took over the Scandinavian pantheon, he also took over an initiatory ritual involving a cave (or a series of nine caves), a maze and a mirror at the center of it.[7] The Japanese Sun Goddess Amaterasu retreats into a cave from which She refuses to reappear, causing the earth to be without a visible sun. She is finally drawn out of Her cave by a sexually explicit dance and sees Her own face in a mirror, thus remembering Her own beauty.

Small figurines of Danish Bronze Age Goddesses have been found which are clothed only in necklaces and sometimes a band or garment around the waist. One of Freya's most notable attributes is the necklace Brisingamen, which may also relate to the turning of the solar wheel. Gefjun has a similar necklace, and there is a myth where Frigg, aided by a dwarf, steals gold from a statue of Odin to make Herself "ornaments."[8] The word *Brisingamen* is usually translated as "ring of fire," from the Old Norse, *brisingr,* "fire," and men, "necklace" or "belt or girdle." There is a saga called the Necklace of the Brisings which contains what little we know about it. The saga is based largely on "Sorla Thattr," a short story in *Flateyjarbok,* c.1400 CE, and we have no evidence that it had earlier antecedents.[9] Yet it is clearly the story of the journey of a Sun Goddess into the dark womb of the earth at winter and Her subsequent return bearing a golden necklace (disk, snake, ring of light). Freya's journey to each of the four directions to obtain it may be a metaphor for the sun's journey through the solstices and equinoxes. It has been suggested that the necklace represents the "circle of the sun's rising and setting points" on the horizon during Her yearly course.[10] Brisingamen is described as "a choker of gold incised with wondrous patterns, a marvel of fluid metal twisting and weaving and writhing."[11] Its description sounds like that of a snake and leads one to wonder if the "wondrous patterns" were runes.

When Sowilo is the rune you have drawn, you hold within you all you need for your own rebirth. As the Sun Goddess, Her light is essential for all life on earth. Perhaps, like Amaterasu, you need only to come out of your cave and laugh to remember your own beauty. The sunwheel is the measure of cyclical time. The sun comes at the end of darkness. Her rising fills the sky and our hearts with hope. When She appears in your runes, it is time to walk away from pain and unhappiness and to embrace the healing powers of play and ritual. Make time to walk in the sunlight. Call on Her to help you see clearly. She opens both our eyes and our hearts, that we may know our own truth and honor it. She is too bright to look at directly, but we see Her reflection all around us. Smile at yourself and find Her in your own mirror.

17. Tiwaz: Spindle

Tiwaz is Frigg's distaff or spindle, a name still used in Sweden today to refer to the stars that form Orion's belt. It is the axis on which the Goddess spins the world. The point of the distaff is the polar star. Most rune books will still tell you that the meaning of this rune is a guiding planet or star, the force of divine order.

The star itself is the jewel of the distaff. Jewel is also the name of Freya's daughter (Hnoss). She is considered "so fair that all precious things (hnossir) are named after Her."[1] The pole star, jewel, is called the navel in the belly of heaven. Here we have a parallel to the navel or omphalos of the Earth Mother, which is significantly considered to be the center of the world. But the story of the Goddess who spins the world is probably far older than our present pole star, Polaris. About four thousand years ago, the star Thubin, in the constellation Draco (the dragon or snake), was the polar star. From the belly of the Earth Mother rises a snake or crowned Goddess, who holds the mystery of rising plant life. Was it then, perhaps, the jewel in the crown of the serpent? Like the Midgaard Serpent that circles the world and holds it together, the snake is associated with world order and the regulation of life. This is cosmic law, not human law. Around Freya's spindle turn the signs of the zodiac, the houses of the sun. Here we have the source of the association of the rune Tiwaz with the law.

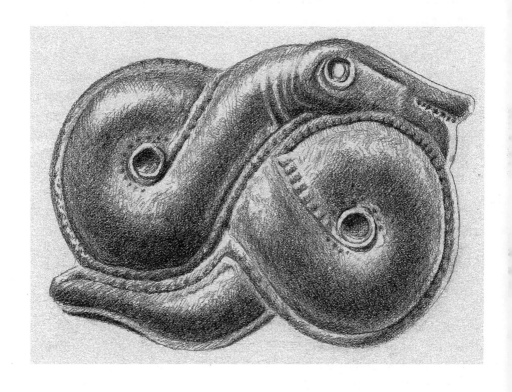

This seventh century bronze snake is a brooch from Öland, Sweden. It may represent the world serpent.

Frigg's distaff is a sign we find together with combs, hooks and spinning wheels on the Bronze Age rock art of Scandinavia. It is shaped exactly like the rune. In Norway, offerings of spinning wheels and flax were made by the Lapps on the altar of the Sun Goddess. They were believed to have taken this custom from the Scandinavians. Offerings to the Finno-Ugaric Goddess Rana-neidda (identified with Frigg) consisted of a spinning wheel or spindle covered with sacrificial blood. In return She was asked to bring the green grass of spring in time to feed the reindeer. She was known as the "greatest of all Goddesses."[2]

One of Freya's names is Horn. As Horn, She is associated with the spinning of flax. Flax was known and used as early as 10,000 years ago. In Scandinavian folktales, maidens were sometimes required to spin flax to gold—a skill which they may have been gifted with by fairies, who also spun sunlight. Marija Gimbutas tells us that spinning, twisting and weaving belonged to a series of Goddesses who survived into late European folklore. Among them were several whose names meant Friday. In Scandinavia, this is Freya's day. On this special day of the Goddess, no other spinning or twisting could be done than Hers.[3] Likewise, no spinning could be done at the season of Yule, Freya's holiday. It was believed that at this critical time of the year, when the sun reached its nadir, the wheels of life came to a standstill. All turning motions, from cart-wheels to churning butter, were forbidden.[4] Even today, all neces-sary spinning and weaving is finished in the weeks preceding the holiday. In Sweden, Frigg is said to spin on Thursday and no other spinning may be done on this day.[5]

The original thread of life was the umbilical cord, that women spun out of the substance of their own bodies, giving life to a child. All spinning and weaving became associated with fate and were considered magical acts. Likewise, the tying and untying of knots held potential for spellwork. Witches were said to cause storm winds by tying knots in a string and blowing on them. A sixth cen-tury CE pendant from Sweden shows Freya with her hair tied in an elaborate knot (see page 21). The knot pattern resembles those associated with harvest knots and sometimes exchanged as love tokens. Elaborate knotwork patterns often appear on Scandinavian metal and stone work.

Here, in Tiwaz, we have both the Goddess as the giver of spinning and weaving and the Divine Spinner creating the order and form of the universe. She both spins the world on Her distaff and is the center or jewel around which it spins. All precious things are a reflection of Her beauty. When you draw Tiwaz, remember that you are a part of the beauty of Her creation. All things are a part of the great pattern She spins in the night sky. See your place in the web. Magic works with the force of cosmic law, never against it. The word *wicca* also means to twist or bend. As witches, we weave the substance of our own lives, working with the natural order of life. When we trust the Goddess and Her universe, we trust ourselves as well. Incorporate Her spinning motion into your spells using tops or dreidels or pinwheels to put you in touch with the natural order in things. Honor Her in the turning of the seasons and the wheel of the year.

18. Berkano: Birch

Berkano is the birch tree, symbol of seasonal rebirth. Even in the most traditional rune lore, this rune remains associated with the Goddess. The seasonal awakening of the birch tree was tied to the awakening and fertility of all other forms of life—from people to crops and animals. Many traditions associated with the birch tree survived into historical times in some form. One such custom is called "birching." Associated with the time of spring planting, it survived even Christianity in many parts of Scandinavia, and is still in practice today. In Norway, children rise early on Shrove-tide and strike the older people, still in bed, with birch branches. From the branches, the first of the year to bud, the adults receive new life and the fruitfulness of spring. The children are rewarded with round buns marked with sun crosses. The branches are then decorated with tinsel, flowers and streamers and a small doll with stiff skirts.[1] Similar forms of birching still exist in Denmark, on Fastelavn (the Monday before Ash Wednesday), and in Sweden as part of the traditions of Good Friday. In Sweden, the branches are cut at the beginning of Lent before the buds of new leaves have opened. They are then decorated with brightly dyed chicken feathers.[2] As a child in Denmark in the late 1950s, I remember being taught to make egg trees, by bringing in bare birch branches and decorating them with both chicken feathers and dyed eggs. The heat of the house soon forced open the tight buds, the first sign of coming spring. By birching, or decorating with birch boughs, the renewal of all related life could be encouraged and insured.

Among the Finns, birch boxes were filled with food and drink at the beginning of spring sowing and taken to a mountain top where they were left as offerings. The next morning, the remaining offerings were eaten by the worshipers accompanied by much drinking and open sexuality.[3] The birch tree held the promise of renewal and fertility that accompanied the returning light of spring. Among the Lapps, a birch pole was the vehicle of shamanic journeys, a form of death and rebirth.[4] Birch boughs also played an important part in the offerings of the Scandinavian Lapps to the Goddess as the Sun Virgin, insuring the health and productivity of the reindeer herds.[5]

One of the early forms of the rune Berkano was a combination of the rune symbol and a row of sun rays. The combination represented the nurturing return of sunlight. The sun's rays are found decorating Swedish rock art and on pendants of amber from Denmark c. 4000 BCE.[6] Amber was regarded as the tears of the Sun Goddess at the time of the Eddas and probably long before that. Her tears were gold on land and amber over water. Translucent and golden, amber was a perfect symbol of Her light, and the rays marked on it represented Her spring energy, which brought renewal and healed the winter torn land. The birch forest represented sunlight to the Balts,[7] and perhaps there were once similar associations in Scandinavia.

The influence of Berkano was felt all the way to Summer Solstice in some parts of Scandinavia, where a birch bough inside the house during the Midsummer bonfire insured future happiness. According to folk songs, lovers in Norway spent the day of the Summer Solstice in the birch groves and swore fidelity to each other under the sun's light.[8] Birch boughs were often part of the decorations of the Midsummer maypole as well.[9]

Berkano is the regenerative power of the Goddess, associated with the returning light of spring. Some scholars identify this Goddess who brings the spring leaves to the trees with Frigg. The Lapps called Her Rana-neidda, and said She was the "greatest of all Goddesses."[10] She is the promise of all new beginnings. Invoke Berkano in your spellwork to bring new growth and fertility to any project. Berkano is the magic of life about to unfold. She is best called on in daylight and at the time of the new moon. If you have ever watched the coming of spring after a long, cold winter, you know the magic of Berkano.

19. Ehwaz: Two Horses

Ehwaz means horse or two horses. This is the ancient Mare Goddess. Her power is that of regeneration and increase. She appeared on the walls of caves in France and Spain as early as the Upper Paleolithic. Several Goddesses have had equine forms. Demeter, Aphrodite and Athena all had horse aspects and Leucippe was the white mare.[1] Rhiannon appeared as a woman on a white horse.[2] The Gallic Epona rode or stood beside a horse or two horses and sometimes held a goblet or bowl that could have held blood.[3] Epona appeared with the Celtic three Matres and was probably one of them. As such, She was associated with fertility.[4] At some later point, these rituals may have begun to include the conferring of kingship through a sacred marriage to the Mare Goddess.[5] Walker reports that ancient kings of Sweden were killed by priestesses of Freya wearing horse masks. She was the twin aspects of death and regeneration.

Horse races were associated with Freya's festival at the Winter Solstice in Sweden and Denmark.[6] The horse races at this time of year became attached to St. Stephen in Sweden, Denmark and England. In England in the sixteenth century, on his feast day, December 26th, horses were raced as fast as possible, watered and then bled for good luck.[7] This suggests the original horse races involved some form of ritual/magical use of blood related to regeneration. The association of the mare with the Goddess of

85

Regeneration is recalled in folktales. There is a folktale from the mountainous district of Germany called the Vosges, about the power of a mare's blood. A young man sets off to recover a lost necklace and sash (or belt) for a princess with the help of a mare and the King of Fishes. He is put in an oven for three days, but is not burned up because he covers his body with the mare's blood. The mare becomes a beautiful young girl, and he chooses her over the princess.[8] According to Graves, an "ecstatic three day horse feast" was celebrated in Denmark through the Middle Ages, until banned by the church. It made use of horse's blood, and was related to the Mare Goddess and the turning of the solar year.[9] Common holiday decorations in both Denmark and Sweden are wooden or cloth horses, in bright colors, painted or embroidered with flowers, hearts, green sprigs and sun symbols.

Some insight into the rituals of the Mare Goddess may be gained by looking at the Roman rituals of the October Horse. As part of a harvest celebration, a horse race was held and one of the team of winning horses was sacrificed. The sacrifice was believed to bring good crops. Blood was also dripped onto the hearth. Blood was saved by the Vestal Virgins and used in the spring to create a purifying smoke for the herds. Frazer believes that the October Horse represented a ritual originally performed on the corn fields at the end of the harvest. He considers the horse to represent both a corn and tree spirit whose blessings must be obtained to insure renewed fertility.[10] Horse sacrifices continued in Norway until the tenth century. In the Middle Ages, witches were said to be able to take the shape of mares.[11]

The number two is also important to an understanding of the concept associated with this rune. It is the power of duplication. The rune sign consists of a hook, the sign for the rune Laguz, and its mirror opposite. It is often translated as two horses. A pair of horses is associated with the dancing of the Sun Goddess from the maze in spring. It is also considered to signify twins. Twins of a sort appear on Scandinavian rock art. They are mirror images of each other and appear to be attached at the head. They remind one of shadow images. The Scandinavian Lapps call the spirit of a shaman *sueje* or shadow. It can take the form of a reindeer, fish, bird or snake.[12] There is a Norse belief that a person's soul can leave the body and take the shape of an animal or appear as the person's double or twin. Called the *fylgja* or follower, it appears when an individual is near death.[13] Traditional rune books often carry this concept of twins a step farther and identify the rune with the Alcis, whom Tacitus identified with the Dioscuri.[14] Scholars have identified some interesting similarities between stories of twins of this type. They often had both cosmic and horse aspects. They were also often associated with waterbirds and sometimes said to be hatched from one egg.[15] The most likely twins represented by this rune, however, are the aspects of the Goddess as winter and summer, life and death, maiden and crone (see Uruz). This aspect survived in folktales as well. The Vosges story of the mare and the princess is one of a type sometimes called the Substitute Bride. Here there is a suitor and two possible brides, one a princess and one who is not what she seems. Another story of the same type is the Little Goose Girl tale, found only in Scandinavia. The story has several different versions. In the Grimms' version, the substitution of the goose girl for the princess is only discovered when the head of a speaking horse is hung on the wall. In both cases, both brides are probably different aspects of the Goddess, sisters or twins, giving way to each other in their turn.

This power is remembered in the Finnish word *jumis*, which means "two things bound together."[16] One of the Goddess' kennings was Hropt, The Binder. Fruits or grains which developed bound together in a double form held power. Sown into a field with the seed, they would bring magical powers of increase to the crop and sometimes protect it as well. With such objects and images, one could invoke the Goddess' magical power to duplicate and multiply life in humans, animals or crops. Jumis also referred to a bundle of bound flax, and was considered to bring luck to weddings.[17]

Ehwaz is the regenerative power of the Mare Goddess. It represents both the power of Her magical fertility and the power of two—horses, twins, objects bound together, to bring about increase.

Use it in your spellwork for all you would see increased or duplicated. She is the power of the mare's blood to revitalize the hearth and to protect the herds. Call on Her for fertility of all kinds, physical fertility or fertility of ideas.

20. Mannaz: Human

Today, Mannaz is usually translated as man. The Old Norse word for the rune was *madhr*. Madhr did not mean man, but rather those born of woman, or humans. The word for a male was not *madhr*, but *wer*. The middle realm of Eddic cosmology was called Mana-heim, or human home. The meaning of this rune was clearly Christianized more than most, becoming a comment on human frailty and mortality. But it was originally an aspect of the Goddess of Death and Rebirth. "The Old Norwegian Rune Rhyme" provides some insight into this rune. It speaks of Mannaz in relation to the claw of the hawk.[1] The hawk was a bird of the Death Goddess, whose message hides in the rune Mannaz. Her sacred birds were also the crows or Valkyries who ate the flesh of the slain. Odin's ravens were undoubtedly Her birds as well. Their names were Thought (or Mind) and Memory.

There are various Eddic myths associated with the acquisition of wisdom, memory and understanding. Mimir was supposed to have been one of the two Aesir (Odin's group) exchanged with the Vanir (older Goddesses and gods) for Freya and Njord. The Vanir killed him and his head was put into the well at the base of Yggdrasill. This then became the source of all wisdom, because Mimir had been the wisest of men. Odin gave an eye for a drink of water from Mimir's well.[2] MacCulloch considers this myth to have been a just-so story explaining the designation of streams as sources of wisdom and knowledge. *Mim* or *Mimi* means the thoughtful one, or to brood over. It is found in the names of several rivers in Sweden and Germany.[3] The triple cauldron, that was the Eddic source of the life giving waters of the earth, was known as *Hvergelmir,* the fount of inspiration and power; *Mimir,* the fount of wisdom and memory; and *Urdarbrunner,* the source of immortality. The cauldrons were tended by the Norns or the three Fates. Think of Shakespeare's image of the three Fates with but one eye between them. Thus, it is the Goddess as Destroyer who rules over the knowledge this rune signifies, which is to be found in Her womb cauldron.

These streams were also associated with sacred groves or trees. Sacred groves were, of course, one of the oldest metaphors for Her womb. In "Svipdagsmal," the world tree was called *Mimameid,* or the tree of Mimir. In folktales, Miming was an aspect of Fate, a wood spirit of great wisdom who was able to increase wealth.[4]

As an aspect of the Fate Goddess, Mimir may simply have meant Mother.[5] Her womb was the source of all resurrection magic, the home of the dead. In Finnish mythology, the Goddess of the Dead was Mana, and Her realm was Manala. When the hero of the Kalevala died he was rescued from Her realm with the help of Mehilainen, the Bee. In Scandinavia, bees were believed to have prophetic powers. From the horns of the four stags who fed at the world tree, honey-dew fell that became the water of the world's rivers. This fluid was hydromel or honey liquid. The original wise blood with which the honey was mixed was the menstrual blood of the Goddess which filled Her triple womb cauldrons.[6]

The Goddess Hel also had a sacred grove where a stream ran. Her sacred trees were elder trees, which were said to be *hellig* (hellish), a medieval Danish word for holy. Her sister was the Midgaard serpent, cast into the ocean by Odin, as Hel was into the Underworld. A line regarding Mannaz in "The Old Icelandic Rune Poem," calls the rune "the adornment of ships."[7] This refers to the snake or dragon helms that decorated Viking ships announcing the coming of death to their foes.

Mannaz is the source of female wisdom, thought, knowledge

and memory. This is not the patriarchal notion of mind separate from flesh. Humanity are those born of woman. Likewise, the source of Her wisdom is Her womb/cauldron, Her life giving waters that run beside the sacred woods. Her knowledge is of the flesh, of the world, of which She and humanity are a part. Female wisdom exists in and of the body. Mannaz is body/spirit/mind combined and as such it is life, which contains within it the knowledge of death.

There is a creation myth where Odin, as a triple god, creates humanity. The three gods walk along the edge of the ocean and see two trees or perhaps blocks of wood, one ash, one elm. The gods give them spirits, minds, the ability to move and blood in their veins. Thus, they create a man and a woman.[8] Even this late patriarchal myth recognizes the need for water and wood; mind, blood and spirit to form life.

Her womb is the source of human life. We all come from Her. But for humanity, life exists as part of a continuum with death, its opposite. She is also the messenger of Death in the same aspect. To Her we shall return. Mannaz is the hawk or crow or raven as the messenger of the Destroyer. It is the flash of Her clawed feet.

Call on Her to help heal the mind/body split of patriarchal culture. Use Mannaz in your spellwork to seek your own deepest wisdom, the wisdom in your bones and blood. Her hidden knowledge is that life and death exist in one another; both are part of what it is to be human.

21. Laguz: Water

Laguz is water, the source of life. It represents the rivers, springs and wells that belonged to Her and also their healing energy. Numerous rivers are named after Her. Streams and wells in particular often retained their associations with the Goddess and their magical attributes long past the advent of Christianity. Swedish writer Monica Sjoo tells us that in Scandinavia the wells were considered to be at their most powerful from Beltaine to the Summer Solstice. In Scandinavia, the cross quarter day of Beltaine was Valbergsmasse Eve. Valberg or Valuburg was an ancient witch (Berchta). Sjoo identifies Her with both Nerthus and Brigid. In Denmark, as in Ireland, many wells were renamed for saints, and continue to be used. As with Brigid's wells, many were particularly powerful in healing eye problems.[1] Remember also that in the Eddas it is an eye that Odin must give to learn the wisdom of Mimir's well.

The magic of certain wells survives in folktales. In a type of German folktale called "Mother Holle" tales, a maid drops a spindle into a well. (Holle is the Goddess of spinning and flax.)[2] She goes into the well to fetch it and finds herself in another land. Here she meets an old woman and is asked to perform tests: to remove bread from the oven; to shake apples from a tree; to shake Mother Holle's bed till feathers fly and people say it is snowing. She returns through the well to her home and is either gifted with magic or showered with gold.[3] In one version as she returns, a hen cries out, "click, clock, clack, our golden girl is back."[4] The well is one of the oldest entrances to the Otherworld. In Baltic folklore, a maid drops her golden ring (symbol of the sun) into a well. It is retrieved by the sons of god (the morning and evening stars).[5]

In still another of Her tales, She brings back the apple of rebirth from the depths of the well where it has fallen at harvest time.[6] Her particular domain includes wells, bogs and marsh lands. Frigg is also associated with such places. The hall where She sits spinning sunlight, or weaving clouds, is called *Fensalir*, variously translated as the hall of mists, the sea or the marsh. A Goddess of the hearth, Holle could sometimes be seen at noon (when the sun was highest) as a beautiful white lady bathing in a lake. When seen, She disappears under water.[7] Wherever Her Wild Hunt ride, the fields will be twice as abundant. The small amount we know of Nerthus also includes the bathing of Her image to renew its powers.

The Old Norse name for this rune suggests to some scholars that it may also have meant leek (ON *laukr*).[8] In the Elder Edda, it is said that leeks spring up where Sunna's feet pass. The leek in question is probably the Lent lily or Goose leek or Asphodel, whose name was corrupted to daffodil.[9] It is yellow with a single circular trumpet—an appropriate flower to rise where the Sun Goddess passes. The asphodel was said to grow on the Elysian fields and was a flower often planted in graveyards. In Wales, people still believe that finding the first daffodil of the season insures a year blessed with wealth and gold.[10] Leek represents the quickening energy of the Goddess that regenerates life. Some of its magic carried over to the common leek as well, which was said both to protect a warrior in battle and to produce a juice that healed sore eyes.[11]

In one thirteenth century Irish version of the story of the "Grain Miracle," most certainly of Celtic origin, the grain is described as growing in the footsteps of the Virgin, much as leeks grow in Sunna's steps.[12] The footsteps of the Goddess appear in Scandinavian rock art and are symbols of Her energy that quickens new life in spring. Feet have long been a symbol of female sexuality. It was a custom to go barefoot into the fields at the rituals of sowing. There is also an Eddic myth in which Skadi chooses a mate among the gods by looking at their feet. Along with footprints, a symbol shaped much like the rune itself appears on Scandinavian rock art, usually accompanied by rays, spindles and sunwheels. Its use is consistent with that of the leek: a symbol of the quickening energy of the Goddess causing new plant life to sprout forth in spring.

Laguz is the symbol of the sacred waters of life. Honor Her presence in rivers, wells and springs. If you are feeling in need of renewal, make time in your life to visit a source of Her life giving waters. Invoke Her magic and healing with the rune. Feel the energy of life rising within you. Use Laguz to bring Her quickening energy to your projects. Use Her water to mark the rune anywhere that you would bring healing, abundance and renewal. Think of Laguz as the mountain stream bursting from its banks in spring. Open yourself to what it brings.

22. Ingwaz: Goddess Ing

Ingwaz or Ing is an aspect of the Goddess Nerthus. Skadi may have been the third aspect. Her people were the Celtic Ingvaeones, who lived in the region between the North Sea and the Baltic. This is the same region where Nerthus was worshiped, and probably referred to Seeland. The earth god Frey was known as Ingvi-Frey, or Ingunar-Frey. This could be translated as either "of Ingun," making Ingun his mother, or as husband or consort of Ingun. (The 'un' is a typical female ending.)[1] But Frey is also said to be the son of Njord (the masculinized version of Nerthus) or of Njord and Nerthus, further evidence that Ing and Nerthus may have been the same Goddess. Frey's worship began in Denmark and spread to Sweden. Scholars speculate that Frey may have been a distant ancestor to the Swedish ruling house, known as the Ynglings. If so, then that distant ancestor was probably seen as a consort of the Goddess, establishing his rule through his relationship to Her in a form of Hieramos Gamos or Sacred Marriage. There is evidence that Freya's temple at Uppsala had priestesses who engaged in sacred sexual rituals.

Several concepts survive in Ingwaz. She is the Progenetrix, source of tribe and kin. She is identified by the symbols of Her vulva, at once both awesome and terrible. This rune holds the power of the Irish sheila-na-gigs, who held open their huge vulvas or pointed to them: source of all life and rebirth and also abode of the dead. Her power and Her sexuality were far too potent and too fearsome to be taken lightly. She was the transformer, who brought the dead back to life, made spirit flesh, the original shapechanger. In Ingwaz is all the primeval worship and fear of the Goddess as the Birthgiving, Devouring Mother. It is interesting that several traditional rune books refer to Ing as a castrated male god. One of Odin's many names was Gelding.

Of particular interest is the diamond or lozenge shape of this sign, sometimes appearing with a dot in the center. It is one of the oldest of Her signs, associated with Her sacred vulva. Two of the alternate forms for this rune are also vulva and birthgiving symbols. The first, commonly used in the Anglo-Saxon rune forms, is a symbol used in weaving throughout much of the world and associated with the Goddess in the position of giving birth. The second is strikingly similar to rock carvings from France that Marija Gimbutas identifies as symbols of the vulva of the Goddess. They are 30,000 years old.[2]

Still another form the rune sign could take was a round circle or a round circle with a dot in the center. This is still the astrological symbol for the sun. The ancient Bird Goddess in Her owl form, as Death Goddess, represented by large round eyes, which are also suns with rays, appears on funerary vases of the Funnel-necked Beaker culture of Neolithic Denmark, c. 3000 BCE.[3] On one vessel, they are accompanied by a series of lozenges shaped like this rune, and by evergreen branches. Her sun eyes can also be found on Bronze Age Scandinavian rock art. What Gimbutas calls Her "radiating divine eyes" is the magic regenerative power that is a fundamental part of the Death Goddess. Her womb is the source of life, the abode of the dead and the promise of rebirth.

The Celtic word for sun, *suil*, comes from the same root as the word for eye, *sulis*. The Finno-Ugaric culture calls the sun the "kindly eye of the heavens."[4] It is no accident that in later times, Odin paid for the knowledge from a sacred well with the loss of an eye, or that St. Lucy (Lucia) is said to have plucked out Her eyes. The enormous round eyes of the Death Goddess, with their associations with both owls and suns, survive to the Bronze Age

The Owl Goddess, with eyes that are also suns, appears on this vase from the Funnel-necked Beaker culture of Neolithic Denmark, c. 3000 BCE.

and can be seen in representations of the Goddess Freya, who is associated with both death and sexuality. This is the rampant, prolific sexuality that brings life, encompasses death and gives rebirth. It is sacred and promiscuous, unruled by any convention set by man.

Cup and ring marks (circles with circular holes or depressions in the center of them) are among the oldest symbols cut into sacred stones. Their shape is the same as that of suns or owl eyes and of the rune. Gimbutas tells us that such marks are both eyes and the source of the tears of the Goddess.[5] The water that gathered in these marks was considered to have intense healing powers. Freya's tears were a kenning for gold or amber, both seen as tears of the sun. The amber of Freya's tears was also considered to have the ability to confer healing.

Still another late Scandinavian myth associates tears with the power of rebirth. In the myth of Baldur's death, it is Loki, in the shape of an old woman sitting in a cave, who alone refuses to cry the tears that Frigg would have used to bring about Her son's rebirth. Frigg is also the Goddess of the Scandinavian pantheon who is appealed to by women at childbirth. Her home is the marshes where spirits of the dead wait to be reborn.

In the rune Ingwaz we have the Goddess Ing as the Great Mother. She is the sacred power of female sexuality. Honor Her by honoring your own sexuality and recognizing it as a source of magic. She is the Birth Giver and She who takes us in at death that we may be reborn through Her. Invoke Her at need—for help in childbirth, for the comfort of Her embrace at death. Her owls see clearly in the darkness and can turn their heads 360 degrees to see in all directions. As one of Her Epiphanies, they see clearly beyond the veil of death. Use Ingwaz in your spellwork to call on the power of their vision. Thank Her for the healing nature of tears.

23. Dagaz: Day

Dagaz means day or the light of day. It may be associated with the springtime awakening or renewal of the sun and the increased hours of daylight. The holiday that marks the Sun Goddess' time of increase in Sweden is called Lady's Day and Lady's Eve[1] (March 25 or Annunciation in the Christian calendar). It is also called Waffle Day—probably a shortening from Var Fru or Our Lady to Vaffer, and eventually to Vaffla or waffle.[2] Sometime during the day, waffles are eaten. To honor the sun, supper is eaten before She sets and all retire without lighting candles, that Hers may be the only light. This is the time of year when the cranes return to Scandinavia. Swedish children are told that the cranes, as Her messengers, will come on Lady's Eve carrying lights and check to see that they are in bed.[3] This day is also considered important in predicting the coming weather. In Belgium, fair weather on the Eve of Lady's Day is thought to bring an abundant harvest.[4] In Belgium, there is also an interesting just-so tale connected with Lady's Day. The wild animals and birds were said to celebrate this day with silence, all but the cuckoo, who went on singing. God then punished the bird by making it wander, without a nest of its own.[5] The cuckoo is sacred to Freya, who as the sun, also wanders, returning in the spring; it is also a bird long associated with oracular prediction. It is widely known as the "messenger of spring."[6] In Germany, if on hearing the cry of the returning cuckoo, money is turned over in one's pocket, it will bring good luck and abundance.[7] But the cuckoo, like the dove, another of Freya's forms, seen or heard at other times of the year, is the call of the Death Goddess or a soul of the dead. In winter, the cuckoo is thought to change shape and become the hawk.[8] Freya could become a hawk/falcon at will by putting on Her magic feathered cloak. Frigg was also considered the Lady of "the hawk's plumage."[9]

As day becomes night or spring becomes winter, both are complementary manifestations of the Goddess. Neither can exist alone. Sacred space is the point where duality meets. It is the recognition that within the circle of the Goddess, what we perceive as opposites are, in fact, simply different points on a continuum. We have in the Spring Equinox that point where light and dark come together in balance and from here the darkness gives way and the daylight grows. Dagaz reminds us of this cycle.

The horizontal hourglass shape of this rune is a symbol often used to represent the labrys or double ax, and also the butterfly. It is most familiar to many of us from its appearance in Crete, where it marks pottery and the life columns that stand near the entrance to the chamber of the priestess at the palace of Knossos, and in similar occurrences on the walls of Tarxien in Malta. But the double ax was a symbol in Scandinavia as well. Over 40 double axes were found in a Swedish temple dating from the Funnel-necked Beaker culture. Among the finds were small axes carved of bone and amber. Like their counterparts in Crete, their purpose was ceremonial in nature.[10] The double ax, an instrument of ritual, like the traditional wiccan tool of the East, the sword or althame, cuts both ways. It is associated with the direction of the rising sun or daylight. In many parts of Europe, moths or butterflies are regarded as witches.[11] They are also, like the dove and cuckoo, both signs of spring and the spirits of the dead. In parts of southern Germany butterflies are believed to bring the souls of the dead to new mothers. The Finno-Ugaric peoples believe that the soul can leave the body as a butterfly while one sleeps, and this accounts for dreams. The Serbians see it as the soul of a witch. If her body is turned around while she sleeps, it will not be able to find her mouth to reenter.[12] Once again, in the butterfly, we have a symbol of the Goddess as transformational.

In Dagaz, we see the survival of the Bird Goddess. Both as a waterbird and other, smaller birds, She is in Dagaz a harbinger of spring and longer days. Yet at the same time, we are made aware of Her power as Balancer of the world's energy, Lady of Transformation. At the moment of the balance point, one thing must always give way to another, which will later give way in its turn—light to dark, spring to fall, birth to death. Dagaz asks that we be aware of the paradoxes in our lives. We live in a culture that divides the world into pairs of polar opposites. Dagaz serves to remind us that within the Craft, the Goddess is all things: life/death/rebirth. As we enter the sacred circle, we move beyond the common boundaries of time and space in which we live our ordinary lives. Here we can perform magic, the magic of our own transformation. To draw Dagaz is to open ourselves to the power of change, directed by our own wills. For witches, Dagaz is a reminder that to manifest change, we must first change our own consciousness. Use Dagaz in your spellwork to help you find the place where opposites connect. Call on Her to help you to deal with change in your life.

24. Othala: Fish

The last of the runes is Othala, the fish—symbol of the fertile womb of the Goddess. Its position here at the end of the runes is an affirmation of the cyclic world view of Goddess oriented cultures. In Her womb is the beginning of life and the promise of rebirth. It is appropriate that both the first rune and the last should represent abundance. In many parts of Scandinavia, fish is eaten at the end of the old year and the beginning of the new and is often associated with luck and well-being.

The eating of Her sacred fish on Fridays, Freya's day, lasted long past its Pagan inception, continuing on in Catholicism until the 1960s. In Sweden, the most important dish, served now on Christmas Eve, is still lutfisk, a traditional fish dish that requires three weeks of soaking and preparing.[1] In Germany, the association of the fish with luck and abundance is clear in the custom of eating carp on New Year's Eve. Folk beliefs hold that if some of the carp's shining scales are put in one's purse at this time, there will be plenty of money for the next twelve months.[2] In other parts of Germany, finding roe in one's fish is said to bring money in the coming year.[3]

There are also interesting associations between the fish and the sun. In the Kalevala, the collected mythology of Finland, the fire that is struck to become the new sun and moon drops in Lake Alue and a fish swallows it.[4] Similarly, the Sun Maiden, Paivatar, rocks

Her fire child in a cradle on the edge of the rainbow. The child falls to earth, where eventually it is swallowed by a fish, which must be captured in a magical net made of flax, grown and spun within two days.[5] The escape made possible through taking fish form and being caught in a net is strikingly similar to the Cretan tale of Minos and Britomartis. Minos pursues Britomartis intending to rape Her. He chases Her for nine months, from sowing to harvest time. She escapes by taking fish form and throwing Herself in the ocean.[6] In some versions, She is saved when She is caught in the fishnets She had invented and given to humanity. She is then known as Britomartis in the east and Dictynna, the Netted One, in the west.[7] String figures, such as Cat's Cradle, were often used in the northern countries to magically net the sun and keep it in the sky a bit longer. The fish is also one of the forms the sun may take to travel across the night sky, or from the point in the western ocean where it sets, to the spot where it rises from the sea in the east.[8] In the Lay of Grimnir, there is a line which reads "and the sun—the fish of the wolf—dances in the water."[9]

The Goddess Nerthus was invoked both for safe sea journeys and for luck at fishing.[10] In many other parts of the world, the Goddess as fish survived quite clearly. Syrian statues of the Goddess show Her holding a cauldron teeming with fish and wearing a skirt decorated with fish.[11] The Chinese Kwan-Yin, Greek Themis and Aphrodite, and Egyptian Mehit all have their fish forms. In Mexico, She can be found both with fish on Her skirts and with the head of a fish. In India, coin purses are still made shaped like fish to bring Her riches. In ancient Malta, pots were decorated with fish scales, necklaces were made of fish vertebrae, and in the Hypogeum, there was found a model of a fish lying on a couch similar to the famous "sleeping lady" found with it. Fish tailed, we know Her in still more parts of the world as both the Goddess and the mermaid. In this form She survived in Scandinavian fairy tales and still sits on Her rock in the Kobenhavn harbor as Anderson's little mermaid.

The fish is the Goddess Herself, Her fertile teeming womb, and the abundance and rebirth that come from Her. Hers is the great mystery, that within the circle of life/death/rebirth every ending is a new beginning. In the rune Othala lies the promise of the Goddess to those who are Her initiates, that the turning of the wheel will once again bring new growth. Call on Her to aid you in your journeys—physical or spiritual. Invoke Her and honor Her with the eating of Her sacred fish. Use the fish as a symbol of increase in your spellwork.

Conclusion

The runes are a potent tool for self knowledge and personal integration. They are a pathway, back to the intuitive, creative parts of ourselves. They offer us a chance to open ourselves to more than one way of knowing; more than a single dimension of knowledge. As we approach both ourselves and the world around us from a fuller perspective, we better understand and appreciate its vast interwoven complexity. We become more fully able to act from the still center of our own wisdom.

In reclaiming the runes, we reclaim a world where such knowledge was valued, the world of the Lady of the Northern Light. Akin to the Great Goddess of Old Europe, She shared many of Her symbols. She was the center and the source; the abundance and rebirth of spring and the storms and death of winter. Her world was cyclical and full of the magic inherent in the dance of life. In the journey from Fehu to Othala, we retrace Her footsteps. Through our use of the runes, we open ourselves to the touch of Her magic. Beneath the surface, Her mysteries have remained, waiting for us to find them. Fragmented, trivialized, forgotten, Her power still beckons.

Now, as we move towards the millennium, the need for a world view that once again values wholistic right brain thinking, such as the runes reveal, is imperative. In Her rituals and Epiphanies, we find the keys to a world where opposites meet as part of a great circle. Through the runes, we can remember our place in that circle and learn to use the wisdom we carry deep in our bones.

Footnotes

Preface

1. Thorsson, *Runelore*, p.11–12.

1. Fehu: Riches

1. Crossley-Holland, *The Norse Myths*, "War of the Aesir and Vanir," p.7.
2. Ibid., p.184.
3. Thorsson, *Futhark, A Handbook of Rune Magic*, p.115.
4. MacCulloch, p.201.
5. Evans, p.155.
6. Frazer, p.106.
7. Crossley-Holland, *The Norse Myths*, p.203.
8. Gimbutas, Marija, *The Language of the Goddess*, p.134.
9. Spicer, p.70-71.
10. Ibid., p.155.
11. Ibid., p.157.
12. Guerber, p.58.

2. Uruz: Aurochs

1. Thorsson, *Futhark, A Handbook of Rune Magic*, p.22.
2. Gimbutas, *The Language of the Goddess*, p.197.
3. "Lay of Hyndla," see Magnusson, p.110 or Crossley-Holland, *The Norse Myths*, p.101.
4. Leach, p.170.
5. Gimbutas, *The Language of the Goddess*, p.302.
6. Graves, p.398–404.
7. Graves, p.404.
8. Ibid., p.401.
9. Ibid., p.400.
10. Note: The tale of Cinderella, the kitchen maid whose place was the ashes of the fireplace, and whose tale was full of animal transformations, is doubtlessly from the same origins. It would have to take place during the time period of a cross quarter day, i.e., between the worlds.
11. Ibid.
12. Note: The series of goose girl tales, involving trials such as spinning straw

to gold, are obviously a related type. Scandinavian folktales (particularly in Norway) often involve a magical black bull associated with a Maid and sometimes a king. The bull leads Her through a series of "trials," and brings Her happiness. Often the bull must be sacrificed. Sometimes the bull is the mother of the Maid reborn in a new form.

13. Graves, p.403.
14. Ibid.

3. Thurisaz: Giant

1. Guerber, p.230.
2. Thorsson, *Futhark, A Handbook of Rune Magic*, p.24. Note: Giant was also a Greek name for the constellation Orion.
3. Guerber, p.230.
4. Thorsson, p.25.
5. Jan, p.318.
6. Frazer, *The Golden Bough*, p.280–285.
7. Thorsson, p.25.
8. Monaghan, *Oh Mother Sun!*, unpublished manuscript.
9. Leach, p.869.
10. Frazer, p.44–47.
11. Cagner, p.46.
12. Spicer, p.156.
13. Cagner, p.48.
14. Ibid.
15. Frazer, p.29-30.
16. Thorsson, *Runelore*, p.184.
17. Spicer, p.217.
18. Ibid., p.101.
19. Ibid., p.217.
20. Cagner, p.81.
21. Walker, *The Woman's Encyclopedia of Myths and Secrets*, p.554.

4. Ansuz: Mouth

1. Random House Dictionary, p.468.
2. Gimbutas, *The Language of the Goddess*, p.15–17.
3. *The Holy Bible, King James Version*, "Gospel according to St.John" 1:1.
4. Guerber, p.39.
5. Ibid.
6. Grimal, p.369.

5. Raidho: Wagon

1. Magnusson, p.47, or Grimal, p.360.

2. Tacitus, p.40.
3. Howard, p.38.
4. Magnusson, p.57. Note: Ships (the counterparts of the wagon) on Scandinavian rock art have keels which also often appear snake like. They are also sometimes portrayed with the heads of stags. An extremely similar drawing of a ship with heads of water birds on both ends and bearing a sunwheel, was recently found in Switzerland, dated Late Bronze Age. ("Europe's First Towns and Entrepreneurs," in Archeology, Vol. 39, #6.)
5. Monaghan, *Oh Mother Sun!,* unpublished manuscript.
6. Spicer, p.63.
7. Ibid., p.26.
8. Matthews, p.147–151.
9. Ibid., p.156–163. Here is a fairly full account of the Troy Dance for those interested. The Cretan labyrinth (Knossos) was widely called city of Troy as recently as 500 years ago. The appearance of the name Truia on an Etruscan vase, which portrays much the same dance as described by Virgil or Tacitus, is interesting, particularly if we remember that the alphabet from which the runes may have come was probably Northern Etruscan. It also leads one to speculate about a possible relationship with the Etruscan Goddess Turan.
10. Ibid.
11. Ibid., p.179.
12. Dexter, p.194, note #103.

6. Kenaz: Torch

1. Shinell, p.15-18.
2. Pausanias, *Description of Greece,* VIII.37.4; *ca.* 150 CE as cited in Dexter, p.116.
3. Frazer, *The Golden Bough,* p.5.
4. Johnson, p.147.
5. Walker, *The Woman's Encyclopedia of Myths and Secrets,* p.400.
6. Ibid.
7. Cagner, p.222.
8. Howard, p.22.
9. MacCulloch, p.201.

7. Gebo: Gift

1. Crossley-Holland, *The Norse Myths,* p.215.
2. MacCulloch, p.181.
3. Crossley-Holland, *The Norse Myths,* from the "Lokasenna," p.164.
4. Leach, p.844.
5. Ibid.
6. Spicer, p.216-217.

7. Berger, p.77.
8. Ibid., p.84-85.
9. Berger, p.86-87.
10. MacCulloch, p.183-184.
11. Guerber, p.47.
12. MacCulloch, p.184.
13. Guerber, p.47.

8. Wunjo: Joy

1. Preble, p.583.
2. MacCulloch, p.307.
3. Ibid., p.307–323.
4. Markale, p.239.
5. Ibid., p.240.
6. Ibid., p.238. Note: It is also interesting that in medieval times the tests that heroes would undergo in Her domain had such names as "Joy of the Court."
7. Ibid., p.239.
8. Walker, *The Woman's Encyclopedia of Myths and Secrets*, p.299.
9. Preble, p.536.
10. Guerber, p.133.
11. Markale, p.79
12. MacCulloch, p.307–323.
13. Ibid., p.313.
14. Guerber, p.18.
15. MacCulloch, p.224–225.
16. Ibid., p.217.

9. Hagalaz: Hail

1. MacCulloch, p.187.
2. Ibid., p.151.
3. Cagner, p.82-83.
4. Spicer, p.55.
5. Ibid.
6. Walker, *The Woman's Encyclopedia of Myths and Secrets*, p.368. (From the Compendium Maleficarum.)
7. Gimbutas, *The Language of the Goddess*, p.319.
8. Spicer, p.212.
9. Ibid.
10. Ibid., p.25.
11. Ibid., p.27.
12. Ibid., p.56.
13. Thorsson, *Futhark, A Handbook of Rune Magic*, p.36.

14. Cagner, p.60.

15. Ibid.

16. Ibid., p.61.

17. "Ukranian Eggs," the Ukranian Gift Shop, Inc., Minn. Minnesota.

18. Ibid.

19. Ibid.

20. Cagner, p.59.

21. Thorsson, p.36.

22. Walker, *The Woman's Dictionary of Symbols and Sacred Objects,* p.67.

23. Ibid.

24. Ibid.

10. Naudhiz: Need-Fire

1. Lippard, p.175.

2. Frazer, *The Golden Bough,* Vol. 2, p.270.

3. Gaynor, p.164.

4. Leach, p.1172.

11. Isa: Ice

1. Guerber, p.238.

2. Ibid.

3. Ibid., p.141.

4. Ibid.

5. Crossley-Holland, *The Norse Myths,* p.195.

6. MacCulloch, p.249.

7. Ibid., p.61, from the "Lay of Grimnir."

8. MacCulloch, p.249.

9. Markale, p.239.

10. Thorsson, *Futhark, A Handbook of Rune Magic,* p.40–41.

11. Guerber, p.181.

12. Jera: Harvest

1. Frazer, *The Golden Bough,* Vol. 2, p.332.

2. Ibid., p.339.

3. Ibid.

4. Ibid., p.343.

5. Cagner, p.45–46.

6. Spicer, p.28.

7. Lippard, p.217.

8. Spicer, p.217.

9. Thorsson, *Runelore,* p.31.

10. Gimbutas, *The Language of the Goddess,* p.16.

11. Ibid., p.242.
12. Ibid.
13. Ibid., p.16.

13. Eihwaz: Yew

1. Murray, p.62.
2. Ibid.
3. Ibid.
4. Howard, p.25.
5. Bogdanovich, p.202.
6. Cagner, p.55.
7. Ibid., p.50.
8. Cagner, p.214. (Note: A similar sun bird is usually hung from the ceiling and referred to as a cuckoo.)
9. Howard, p.24–25.

14. Perthro: Lots

1. Thorsson, *Futhark, A Handbook of Rune Magic*, p.46–47.
2. Guerber, p.166.
3. Ibid., p.166–170.
4. MacCulloch, p.301.
5. Guerber, p.166–170.
6. Gimbutas, *The Language of the Goddess*, p.286–287.
7. Holmberg, p.253.
8. Walker, *The Woman's Encyclopedia of Myths and Secrets*, p.934.
9. Ibid.
10. Ibid.
11. Spicer, p.23-24.
12. Ibid.
13. Spicer, p.23-24.
14. Ibid.
15. Howard, p.42.
16. Guerber, p.171.
17. Howard, p.34.

15. Elhaz: Elk

1. Thorsson, *Futhark, A Handbook of Rune Magic*, p.48. (GO)
2. Holmberg, p.224.
3. Grimal, p.426.
4. Markale, p.108.
5. Ibid.
6. Johnson, p.218-220.

7. Ibid.
8. Markale, p.110.
9. Ibid.
10. Guerber, p.173.
11. Ibid.
12. Ibid., p.173–174.

16. Sowilo: Sun Goddess

1. Markale, p.240.
2. From the Vafthrudnismal, see Crossley-Holland, *The Norse Myths,* p.78.
3. Phone conversation with Monaghan, also in an as yet unpublished book, *Oh Mother Sun!*
4. Matthews, p.147-151.
5. A good version appears in Crossley-Holland, *The Norse Myths,* p.9-14 (based on the Prose Edda).
6. Holmberg, p.223–225.
7. Howard, p.14–15.
8. MacCulloch, p.174–177.
9. (Beyond a brief mention in 978 CE, in the Husdrapa, by Ulfuggason) Crossley-Holland, *The Norse Myths,* p.202.
10. Jones, "Circles of Earth, Circles of Heaven," in *Voices from the Circle,* p.46.
11. Crossley-Holland, *The Norse Myths,* p.65.

17. Tiwaz: Spindle

1. MacCulloch, p.120.
2. Holmberg, p.225.
3. Gimbutas, *The Language of the Goddess,* p.68.
4. Walker, *The Woman's Encyclopedia of Myths and Secrets,* p.1074.
5. MacCulloch, p.174–177.

18. Berkano: Birch

1. Spicer, p.151–152. (Note the similarity here to images of Brigid carried in Ireland at Imbolc.)
2. Ibid., p.213.
3. Ibid., p.228–229.
4. Howard, p.31.
5. Holmberg, p.224.
6. Gimbutas, *The Language of the Goddess,* p.300.
7. Jan, p.328.
8. Spicer, p.154.
9. Spicer, p.216.
10. Holmberg, p.249.

19. Ehwaz: Two Horses

1. Leach, p.504.
2. Markale, p.88–92.
3. Ibid.
4. Leach, p.346.
5. Monaghan, *The Book of Goddesses and Heroines,* p.110.
6. Berger, p.109–110.
7. Berger, p.110; see also Walker, *The Woman's Encyclopedia of Myths and Secrets,* p.414.
8. Markale, p.90–91.
9. Graves, p.384.
10. Frazer, *The Golden Bough,* p.64–67.
11. Walker, p.412–413.
12. Holmberg, p.285.
13. MacCulloch, p.233.
14. Thorsson, *Futhark, A Handbook of Rune Magic,* p.59.
15. Leach, p.314–315.
16. Gimbutas, p.166.
17. Ibid.

20. Mannaz: Human

1. Thorsson, *Runelore,* p.101.
2. Crossley-Holland, *The Norse Myths,* p.184. (sources: Voluspa and Sturluson)
3. MacCulloch, p.67–70.
4. Ibid.
5. Walker, *The Woman's Encyclopedia of Myths and Secrets,* p.154.
6. Ibid.
7. Thorsson, *Runelore,* p.103.
8. Guerber, p.12.

21. Laguz: Water

1. Sjoo, "Holy Wells," in *WomanSpirit,* Spring, 1984.
2. Leach, p.500.
3. Ibid.
4. Exner, p.15-17.
5. Jan, p.327.
6. Gimbutas, *The Language of the Goddess,* p.319–320.
7. Leach, p.500.
8. Thorsson, *Futhark, A Handbook of Rune Magic,* p.62–63.
9. Leach, p.274.
10. Ibid.

11. Leach, p.612.
12. Berger, p.98.

22. Ingwaz: Goddess Ing

1. MacCulloch, p.112.
2. Gimbutas, *The Language of the Goddess*, p.99.
3. See plate 38 a, b, Crawford, *The Eye Goddess*, p.109 and Gimbutas, p.56–57.
4. Holmberg, p.223.
5. Gimbutas, *The Language of the Goddess*, p.61.

23. Dagaz: Day

1. Spicer, p.213.
2. Ibid., p.214.
3. Ibid.
4. Ibid., p.6.
5. Ibid.
6. Leach, p.267.
7. Ibid.
8. Gimbutas, *The Language of the Goddess*, p.195.
9. MacCulloch, p.174–177.
10. Gimbutas, *The Civilization of the Goddess*, p.268.
11. Leach, p.176.
12. Ibid.

24. Othala: Fish

1. Spicer, p.221.
2. Ibid., p.85.
3. Ibid., p.84.
4. Lonnrot, p.314.
5. Monaghan, *Oh Mother Sun!*, unpublished manuscript.
6. Graves, p.402. This is part of the seasonal transformation of animals discussed in Uruz and in Graves 398-403. (Artemis, Dictynna, Britomartis, Astergatis, Aegea, Cronis, Rhea)
7. Monaghan, *The Book of Goddesses and Heroines*, p.51.
8. Leach, p.1172.
9. Crossley-Holland, *The Norse Myths*, p.61.
10. Magnusson, p.75.
11. Weiss, see figs. 42 & 90, Zimri-Lim Palace, Mari, c.1800 (among others).

Summaries of Rune Meanings

Words, isolated from their original context, then interpreted in the light of a vastly different world view, can lose their original meaning and intent. The meaning of the runes can only be restored within the context of a Goddess centered universe. It is important to understand such a world view, to understand the true meaning of the runes. The *Summaries of Rune Meanings,* provided as an aid to your own readings, are appropriate only within that context. They cannot hope to express the full complexity of the runic concepts dealt with in the text, but are given only to act as a quick source of reference.

Fehu: wealth, luck, abundance, divination, prophecy

Uruz: energy source, underlying connections, changing form, transformation

Thurisaz: awakening, growth, new possibilities, breaking down of boundaries

Ansuz: inspiration, speech, voice of the Goddess, true vision, power of words and naming

Raidho: dance of life, underlying pattern, maze, trance state, larger perspective

Kenaz: vital fire of life, torch, hearth, ever burning flame, power to create your reality

Gebo: gifts of the Goddess, blessings, power to create from within yourself, exchange of energy

Wunjo: domain of the Queen of the Dead and Her snakes, secret knowledge, communication with foremothers, joy of life

Hagalaz: harmony, balance, strength, protection, wild power in untamed nature

116

Naudhiz: distress, confusion, conflict, and the power of the will to overcome them, major self-initiated change

Isa: benevolent aspect of crone/death/winter, time to turn inward, wait for what is to come

Jera: good harvest, time of peace and happiness, fruitful season

Eihwaz: letting go, necessary ending, release, death as natural part of the cycle of life

Perthro: knowledge of future patterns, determining the future, continuum of time, determining your path

Elhaz: continuity and nurturance of the life force, invocation of Her protection, continuance, particularly through kinship

Sowilo: She who gives birth to Herself, power of self-renewal, healing power of play and ritual, self-knowledge

Tiwaz: the Divine Spinner, creation of form and order in the universe, power to weave the pattern of your own life

Berkano: regenerative power and light of spring, renewal, promise of new beginnings, new growth

Ehwaz: magical increase of fertility, power of two to bring increase, physical fertility, fertility of ideas

Mannaz: female wisdom, deep wisdom held in the body, mind and body as one, knowledge, memory

Laguz: Her sacred life giving waters, quickening energy, the healing power of renewal

Ingwaz: sacred power of female sexuality, vulva, Birthgiver and Devouring Mother

Dagaz: balance point, the place where opposites meet, power of change directed by your own will, transformation

Othala: in the ending is the beginning, the womb of the Goddess, aid in spiritual and physical journeys, source of increase and abundance

Glossary of Northern Goddesses

Angr-boda: A giant, mother of Hel and the Fenris wolf, She lives in the Ironwood, may be related to Skadi.

Berchta, Perchta: A Germanic Goddess, wanders through the fields during the twelve days of Christmas bringing them fertility and also causing harm; has bulging eyes, wrinkles and tangled hair.

Freya: Member of Vanir who becomes part of pantheon of Aesir. Her emblem is the necklace Brisingamen. Hers is the magic of reading runes, trancing and casting spells. She owns a falcon cloak, takes dove form, rides in a chariot drawn by two black lynx and rides a boar. As the leader of the Valkyries, She takes half those slain in battle and is traditionally associated with death and sexuality. She retains sun symbolism; cries tears of gold and amber; Her day is Friday; Jul is Her holiday; She is the mother of Hnoss.

Frigg: Member of the Aesir, married to Odin. Called Lady of the Hawk Plumage and Mother of the gods. She is the Goddess of childbirth, retains sun symbolism, is an aspect of fate. Her hall was Fensalir.

Fulla: An attendant of Frigg and one of Her aspects, She carries the coffer of life and death. Her name means abundance and She carries aspects of sexuality and fate.

Gefn, Gefjun: The All-Giver, She is associated with sowing of fields, crop and human fertility, celebrated with wagon rituals and plough rites at the New Year. As the Danish Goddess, She turned Her sons to oxen and ploughed Jutland from Sweden. An aspect of fate, She is called on in oath taking. Unwed women go to Her hall at death. She owns a shining necklace and is an aspect of Freya.

Gollveig: Her name means Gold Might. A member of Vanir, She was thrown three times in the fire in Odin's hall and emerged whole and shining. The forms of magic attributed to Freya belong to this aspect of Her.

Hel: Goddess of Death and the Underworld which takes Her name, She is the daughter of Angr-boda, sister of the Midgaard Serpent.

Hnoss: The daughter of Freya, Her name means Jewel.

Holda, Holle, Holla: These are German names for a Goddess who rules the weather—sunshine, snow, rain; dwells at the bottom of a well; rides a wagon; gives the gift of flax and spinning.

Horn: She is an aspect of Freya as Giver of Flax.

Huldra: A Germanic Goddess whose maidens are wood nymphs or elves and sing magical songs in the mountains where they live. She and they, have cows tails. In some parts of Scandinavia, She was considered the same as Nerthus.

Hyrrokin: A giant, She rides a wolf with a bridle of snakes. She launches Balder's funeral boat with a mighty shove.

Idun: A late Eddic Goddess who keeps the golden apples of immortality.

Ingun: Mother or consort of Frey, She may have been a face of Nerthus. She is the Progenetrix, Birthgiver and Devourer.

Lucia: Saint Lucia was probably of northern Italian origin. Her holiday in Sweden is the old calendar Winter Solstice. Crowned with light, She moves at dawn across ice-bound lakes and brings food for the poor.

Mana: The Finnish Death Goddess of the Kalevala, Her realm is called Manala.

Mardoll: An aspect of Freya, Her name means shining over the sea.

Nerthus: She is the oldest Scandinavian Goddess whose name came down to us. She lived in a grove on a sacred island. Once a year She traveled across the land in a wagon bringing a season of peace and plenty. When She tired, She returned to Her island and was bathed in a lake by slaves who were later drowned.

Norns: The Eddic name for the three fates.

Rana-neidda: A Lapp Goddess, She brings spring renewal and grass for the reindeer.

Saga: The sagas or songs of history are named for Her. She lived in Sokvabek, a crystal hall, and drank daily from the river of time with Odin.

Scatach: A Lapp Goddess, Her name means She who strikes fear.

Sif: An aspect of Freya, Her golden hair was cut off and replaced with hair of gold made by the dwarfs.

Skadi: A giant, probably of Finnish origin, She became part of the Aesir pantheon and was married to Uller and Niord. She may have been the third aspect of Nerthus. Goddess of winter and death, She brings the snow which insures a good harvest and leads the Wild Hunt. The wolf and poisonous snake are sacred to Her.

Syr: An aspect of Freya as the Golden Sow.

Thorgerd: A Finnish Goddess later called a troll, She used magic to call thunder, lightning and hail.

Valkyries: Called battle maidens, they have raven and swan forms, choose among the slain and bring fertility to the earth.

Bibliography

Achterberg, Jeanne. *Woman As Healer.* Boston: Shambhala, 1990.

Asbjornsen, Peter Christen and Moe, Jorgen. *Norwegian Folktales.* New York: Pantheon Books.

Berger, Pamela. *The Goddess Obscured.* Boston: Beacon Press, 1985.

Bogdanovich, Peter. *A Year and A Day Engagement Calandar 1992.* New York: Overlook Press, 1991.

Booss, Claire. *Scandinavian Folk and Fairy Tales.* New York: Avnel Books, 1984.

Branson, Brian. *Gods of the North.* New York: Thames and Hudson, 1964.

Brennan, Martin. *The Stars and the Stones.* London: Thames and Hudson, 1983.

Budge, E. A. Wallis. *The Gods of the Egyptians.* New York: Dover, 1969.

Cagner, Ewert. *Swedish Christmas.* Gothenburg, Sweden: Tre Tryckare, 1955.

Crawford, Osbert Guy Stanhope. *The Eye Goddess.* London: Phoenix House, 1957.

Crossley-Holland, Kevin, ed. *The Faber Book of Northern Folktales.* London: Faber and Faber, Ltd., 1980.

Crossley-Holland, Kevin. *The Norse Myths.* New York: Pantheon Books, 1980.

Davidson, Hilda Ellis and Geller, Peter. *The Chariot of the Sun.* New York: Praeger, 1969.

Davidson, Hilda Ellis. *Myths and Symbols of Pagan Europe, Early Scandinavian and Celtic Religions.* New York: Syracuse University Press, 1988.

Davidson, Hilda Ellis. *Scandinavian Mythology.* New York: Hamlyn, 1969.

Dexter, Miriam Robbins. *Whence the Goddesses: A Source Book.* New York: Pergamon Press, 1990.

Dolphin, Deon. *Rune Magic.* North Hollywood, CA: Newcastle Publishing Co., 1987.

Dronke, U., ed. *The Poetic Edda.* London: Oxford University Press, 1969.

Durdin-Robertson, Lawrence. *The Year of the Goddess.* Wellingborough: The Aquarian Press, 1990.

Eliade, Mircea, ed. *The Encyclopedia of Religion.* New York: Macmillan, 1987.

Eogan, George. *Knowth.* London: Thames and Hudson, 1986.

"Europe's First Towns and Entrepreneurs," in *Archeology.* Volume 39, #6.

Evans, Emyr Estyn. *Irish Heritage.* Dundalk: Dundalgan Press, 1963.

Exner, Carol. "The Goddess in Fairytales," in *WomanSpirit,* Spring, 1983.

Faulkes, Anthony. *Snorri Sturluson, Edda, Prologue and Glyfaginning.* Oxford: Clarendon Press, 1982.

Frazer, James G. *The Golden Bough.* New York: Avnel Books, 1981.

Frazer, James (translator). *Ovid's Fasti.* Cambridge: Loeb Classical Library, 1959.

Gaynor, Elizabeth. *Scandinavian Living Design.* New York: Stewart, Tabori & Chang, 1987.

Gimbutas, Marija. *The Balts.* New York: Praeger, 1963.

Gimbutas, Marija. *The Civilization of the Goddess: The World of Old Europe*. New York: HarperSanFrancisco, 1991.

Gimbutas, Marija. *The Goddesses and Gods of Old Europe*. Los Angeles: University of California Press, 1982.

Gimbutas, Marija. *The Language of the Goddess*. New York: Harper & Row, 1989.

Glob, P. V. *The Bog People*. New York: Ballantine Books, 1969.

Glob, P. V. *The Mound People*. New York: Cornell University Press, 1974.

Graves, Robert. *The White Goddess*. New York: Farrar, Straus and Giroux, 1949.

Grimal, Pierre, ed. *Larousse World Mythology*. New York: Gallery Books, 1989.

Guerber, H. A. *The Norsemen*. London: Bracken Books, 1986.

Holmberg, Uno. *Mythology of All Races*, Volume IV: Finno-Ugaric, Siberian. New York: Cooper Square Publishers, 1964.

Howard, Michael. *The Magic of the Runes*. Wellingborough: The Aquarian Press, 1980.

Jan, Machal. *Mythology of All Races*, Volume III: Baltic (Celtic and Slavic). New York: Cooper Square Publishers, 1964.

Johnson, Buffie. *Lady of the Beasts*. San Francisco: Harper & Row, 1988.

Jones, Prudence and Matthews, Caitlin, eds. *Voices from the Circle*. Wellingborough: The Aquarian Press, 1990.

Kelly, Mary. *Goddesses and Their Offspring*. Bingham, New York: Roberson Center for Arts and Sciences, 1986.

Krause, Ernst. "The Northern Origin of the Story of Troy," in *Open Court*. August, 1918.

Krupp, Dr. E. C. *In Search of Ancient Astronomies*. New York: Doubleday and Co., 1978.

Kuhn, Herbert. *The Rock Pictures of Europe*. London: Sidgwick and Jackson, 1956.

"Labyrinths and the Picture of Tragliatella," in *Open Court.* August (1989): 449.

Leach, Maria, ed. *Funk & Wagnalls Standard Dictionary of Folklore, Mythology, and Legend.* New York: Harper & Row, 1984.

Line, David and Julia. *Fortune Telling By Runes.* Wellingborough: The Aquarian Press, 1984.

Lippard, Lucy R. *Overlay.* New York: Pantheon Books, 1983.

Lonnrot, Elias. *The Old Kalevala and Certain Antecedents.* (translated by Francis Peabody Magou) Cambridge: Harvard University Press, 1969.

MacCulloch, Canon John A. *Mythology of All Races*, Volume II: Eddic. New York: Cooper Square Publishers, 1964.

Magnusson, Magnus. *Hammer of the North.* New York: G. P. Putnam's Sons, 1976.

Markale, Jean. *Women of the Celts.* Rochester, Vermont: Inner Traditions International, Ltd., 1986.

Matthews, W. H. *Mazes and Labyrinths, Their History and Development.* New York: Dover Publications, Inc., 1970.

Mayani, Zacharie. *The Etruscans Begin To Speak.* New York: Simon and Schuster, 1962.

Monaghan, Patricia. *The Book of Goddesses and Heroines.* New York: E. P. Dutton, 1981.

Monaghan, Patricia. *The Book of Goddesses and Heroines.* St. Paul: Llewellyn Publications, 1990.

Monaghan, Patricia. *Oh Mother Sun!* unpublished manuscript.

Murray, Liz and Murray, Colin. *The Celtic Tree Oracle.* New York: St. Martin's Press, 1988.

O'Flaherty, Wendy. *Other People's Myths: The Cave of Echoes.* New York: Macmillan, 1988.

O'Kelly, Michael J. *Newgrange.* London: Thames and Hudson, 1982.

Osborn, Marijane and Longland, Stella. *Rune Games*. London: Routledge and Kegan Paul, 1982.

Pennick, Nigel. *Earth Harmony*. London: Century Hutchinson Publishing Group, 1987.

Preble, Robert. *Britannica World Language Dictionary*. New York: Funk and Wagnalls, 1958.

River, Lindsay and Gillespie, Sally. *The Knot of Time*. New York: Harper & Row, 1987.

Ross, Anne. *The Pagan Celts*. New Jersey: Barnes and Noble, 1986.

Shepard, Paul and Sanders, Barry. *The Sacred Paw: The Bear in Nature, Myth and Literature*. Viking Penguin Books, 1985.

Shinell, Grace. "To Hell and Back Again, Towards A Feminist Metaphysics," in *WomanSpirit*, Spring, 1980.

Sjoo, Monica. "Holy Wells," in *WomanSpirit*, Spring, 1984.

Spicer, Dorothy Gladys. *Festivals of Western Europe*. New York: The H. W. Wilson Co., 1958.

Starhawk. *The Spiral Dance*. San Francisco: Harper & Row, 1979.

Stein, Jess. *The Random House Dictionary*. New York: Ballantine Books, 1978.

Sturluson, Snorri. *The Prose Edda*. (translated by Arthur Brodeur) New York: The American Scandinavian Foundation, 1929.

Tacitus. *Germania*. (translated by H. Mattingly) New York: Penguin Books, 1948.

Terry, Patricia, trans. *Poems of the Vikings: The Elder Edda*. New York: Bobbs-Merrill Company, Inc., 1969.

Thorsson, Eldred. *Futhark, A Handbook of Rune Magic*. York Beach, Maine: Samuel Weiser, Inc., 1984.

Thorsson, Eldred. *Runelore*. York Beach, Maine: Samuel Wieser, Inc., 1987.

Turville-Petre, E. O. G. *Myth and Religion of the North*. New York: Holt, Rinehart, Winston, 1964.

Walker, Barbara G. *The I Ching of the Goddess.* San Francisco: Harper & Row, 1986.

Walker, Barbara G. T*he Woman's Dictionary of Symbols and Sacred Objects.* San Francisco: Harper & Row, 1988.

Walker, Barbara G. *The Woman's Encyclopedia of Myths and Secrets.* New York: Harper & Row, 1983.

Weiss, Harvey. *Elba to Damascus.* Washington DC: Smithsonian Institute, 1985.

West, John Anthony. *Serpent in the Sky.* New York: The Julian Press, 1987.

Wilkinson, Sir J. Gardner. *The Ancient Egyptians.* New York: Bracken Books, 1988.

Wosien, Maria-Gabriele. *Sacred Dance.* New York: Thames and Hudson, 1974.

About the Author

Susan Gitlin-Emmer is an educator, artist, activist and witch. She lives in the San Fernando Valley, north of Los Angeles, California, where she teaches classes in Feminist Witchcraft, the contemporary practice of Goddess religion. She works with a group of women who combine their psychic healing and magic skills through consulting, rituals, and workshops.